Contemporary Techniques in Architecture

Guest-edited by Ali Rahim

W WILEY-ACADEMY

Architectural Design
Vol 72   No 1 January 2002

ISBN 0-470-84320-9
Profile No 155

Editorial Offices
International House
Ealing Broadway Centre
London W5 5DB
T: +44 (0)20 8326 3800
F: +44 (0)20 8326 3801
E: architecturaldesign@wiley.co.uk

Editor
Helen Castle
Executive Editor
Maggie Toy
Production
Famida Rasheed & Amie Tibble
Art Director
Christian Küsters ↘ CHK Design
Designer
Owen Peyton Jones ↘ CHK Design
Picture Editor
Famida Rasheed

Advertisement Sales
01243 843272

Editorial Board
Denise Bratton, Adriaan Beukers,
André Chaszar, Peter Cook,
Max Fordman, Massimiliano
Fuksas, Anthony Hunt, Charles
Jencks, Jan Kaplicky, Robert
Maxwell, Jayne Merkel, Monica
Pidgeon, Antoine Predock,
Leon van Schaik

Contributing Editors
Craig Kellogg
Jeremy Melvin

Ali Rahim would like to thank
Mr and Mrs JR Rahim and Hina
Jamelle for their support.

Photo Credits
AD Architectural Design

Abreviated positions
b=bottom, c=centre, l=left, r=right

pp 4–8 © Ali Rahim, Contemporary Architecture Practice; pp 13–16 MIT/Emergent Design Group; pp 17–19 © Servo; pp 20–27 © Preston Scott Cohen; p 28 © Bernard Cache, photo Patrick Renault and Marie Combes; pp 30–1 courtesy Bernard Cache, design: Bernard Cache and Patrick Beauce, photos © Patrick Renault and Marie Combes; pp 34–41 © OCEAN North; pp 42–5 © Kristina Shea; pp 46–51 © Cecil Balmond, Ove Arup; pp 52–63 © Ali Rahim, Contemporary Architecture Practice; pp 64–71 courtesy Greg Lynn, Form; pp 72–6 © Johan Bettum; pp 77, 79, 80 & 81 © Kolatan/MacDonald Studio; pp 78, 82 & 83, photos: © Michael Moran; pp 84–92 © Foreign Office Architects; p 94 courtesy ESI Group.

AD +
pp 98–9+ & 101(cr)+ photos: © Paul Warchol Photography, Inc; pp 100–101+ © Winka Dubbledam, Archi-Tectonics; p 102(t)+ © Albert Szabo; p 102(b)+ photo: © Frieda Sorber 1998; p 104+ courtesy The Architects' Journal; p 105+ © Festo Corporate Design; p 106(t)+ courtesy of the European Space Agency; p 108(l)+ photo: © Werner Baser, courtesy Canadian Centre for Architecture, Montréal; p 108(r)+ 2001 The Museum of Modern Art, New York; p 109(l)+ Collection Canadien d'Architecture/Canadian Centre for Architecture, Montréal, © Ezra Stoller; p 109(r)+ Collection Canadien d'Architecture/Canadian Centre for Architecture, Montréal, © Detlef Mertins; p 110(l)+ & 110(r)+ © 2001 Kay Fingerie and The Museum of Modern Art, New York; p 111(t)+ in the collection of the Canadian Centre for Architecture, Montreal, courtesy The Museum of Modern Art, New York; p 111(b)+ Mies van der Rohe Archive, gift of the architect, © The Museum of Modern Art, New York; pp 113(t)+, 114+,115(t)+ & 116(t)+ courtesy Rafael Viñoly Architects; p 113(b)+, 115(b)+, 116(b)+ & 117 © Jeff Goldberg\Esto; pp 118–23+ © S333; p 126+ © Charlotte Wood; p 127 courtesy Burd Haward Marsden Architects.

© 2002 John Wiley & Sons Limited.
All rights reserved.

No part of this publication may be
reproduced, stored in a retrieval
system, or transmitted, in any
form or by any means, electronic,
mechanical, photocopying,
recording, scanning or otherwise,
except under the terms of the
Copyright Designs and Patents Act
1988 or under the terms of a
licence issued by the Copyright
Licensing Agency, 90 Tottenham
Court Road, London UK, W1P 9HE,
without permission in writing of the
publisher.

Cover image
© Ali Rahim – Contemporary
Architecture Practice

Subscription Offices UK
John Wiley & Sons Ltd.
Journals Administration Department
1 Oldlands Way, Bognor Regis
West Sussex, PO22 9SA
T: +44 (0)1243 843272
F: +44 (0)1243 843232
E: cs-journals@wiley.co.uk

Subscription Offices USA and Canada
John Wiley & Sons Ltd.
Journals Administration Department
605 Third Avenue
New York, NY 10158
T: +1 212 850 6645
F: +1 212 850 6021
E: subinfo@wiley.com

Annual Subscription Rates 2002
Institutional Rate: UK £160
Personal Rate: UK £99
Student Rate: UK £70
Institutional Rate: US $240
Personal Rate: US $150
Student Rate: US $105

AD is published bi-monthly.
Prices are for six issues and include
postage and handling charges.
Periodicals postage paid at Jamaica,
NY 11431. Air freight and mailing in the
USA by Publications Expediting Services
Inc, 200 Meacham Avenue, Elmont,
NY 11003

Single Issues UK: £22.50
Single Issues outside UK: US $36.00
Order two or more titles and postage
is free. For orders of one title add
£2.00/US $5.00. To receive order
by air please add £5.50/US $10.00

Postmaster
Send address changes to AD Publications
Expediting Services, 200 Meacham Avenue,
Elmont, NY 11003

Printed in Italy. All prices are subject
to change without notice.
[ISSN: 0003-8504]

4	Editorial *Helen Castle*
5	Introduction *Ali Rahim*
9	Deleuze and the Use of the Genetic Algorithm in Architecture *Manuel DeLanda*
13	Emergent Structural Morphology *Peter Testa and Devyn Weiser*
17	Interactive Opportunities *David Erdman, Marcelyn Gow, Ulrika Karlsson, Chris Perry/Servo*
20	Toroidal Architecture *Preston Scott Cohen*
28	Gottfried Semper: Stereotomy, Biology and Geometry *Bernard Cache*
34	Vigorous Environment *Michael Hensel and Kivi Sotamaa/OCEAN North*
42	Creating Synthesis Partners *Kristina Shea*
46	The Digital and the Material *Michael Weinstock with Cecil Balmond*
52	Potential Performative Effects *Ali Rahim*
64	Predator *Greg Lynn*
72	Skin Deep - Polymer Composite Materials in Architecture *Johan Bettum*
77	'Lumping' *Sulan Kolatan and William MacDonald*
84	Roller-Coaster Construction *Alejandro Zaera-Polo/Foreign Office Architects*
93	Virtually Crash Testing the Box *Jeff Turko*
95	Biographies

Contemporary Techniques in Architecture

Guest-edited by Ali Rahim

98+	Interior Eye: Archi-Tectonics, Aida Hair Salon *Craig Kellogg*
102+	Engineering Exegesis: Lightweight Structures *Bas Veldman and Oscar Mölder*
108+	Beat the Devil *Diane Lewis*
113+	Building Profile: Climate Prediction Center *Jeremy Melvin*
118+	Practice Profile: S333 *Lucy Bullivant*
124+	Highlights from Wiley-Academy
125+	Book Reviews
126+	Site Lines

The sequel to Ali Rahim's highly successful *Contemporary Processes in Architecture* issue of AD, this title is no mere add-on or opportunistic follow on. It was conceived in tandem with the first project. Discussed in abstract with Rahim in its early stages I envisaged it dealing with a discrete area of practice like that of processes, which dealt almost solely with the generative and the creative design stage. Techniques, however, as a 'means of achieving one's purpose', specifically in a contemporary context have not proved nearly so neat. Though the issue reproduces projects, such as the Yokohama Port Terminal and the O/K Apartments, in which the employment of innovative production methods have enabled the dreams of the avant-garde to become a reality, new technologies alone are not the main thrust of the publication. It is to Rahim's credit that he has insisted that this theme must be concerned with far more than 'the technical' and must truly reflect the interface between architecture and contemporary culture — in his own words 'a complex feedback loop'. Δ

In this issue of *Architectural Design* contributors explore the relationship between techniques, and cultural and architectural production, and investigate the connections that link them. Contemporary techniques are part of a complex feedback loop. They produce new effects which act on or influence an object, affecting human behaviour and technical performance. This transforms culture through replication and produces new and different effects – new techniques.

Contemporary techniques thus constitute the beginning, and the end, of the loop, which is perpetuated and proliferated by technology. This proliferation is contingent on an understanding of technology activated within its cultural context. The interaction between technology and the user creates the possibility for qualitative cultural transformation through the transmission of behaviours that are replicated.

Ostensibly contemporary techniques' contribution lies in the progress of a culture that is driven by a machinic process which self-organises, bifurcates and produces new emergent results. It is experimental architects' use of current techniques to generate these organisational processes that enables them to understand the possibilities contained with the design process. This sees the replacement of determinist notions of causality with nonlinear, bottom-up systemic processes which produce emergent effects. For example, Manuel Delanda exploits the possibilities contained within the genetic algorithm, in which evolutionary simulations replace design and software breeds new forms. He emphasises the need to create fertile spaces that are 'rich enough' for the evolutionary results to be exceptional, and sufficiently open-ended to make it impossible for the designer to consider all possible configurations in advance.

The relationship between techniques and material objects is potentially that of dynamic organisations which challenge the stasis of the formal object. For example, Kristina Shea has created a prototype system of synthesis techniques called eifForm that relates material objects to aspects of geometry, topology and principles of structural engineering. This has the effect of moving the work away from material specialisations and restrictions, or specific applications, and allows for interaction with dynamic processes that contribute to the rapid generation of design alternatives that are void of material restraints. These new computational techniques lead to the creation

of innovative, free-form, discrete structures and the incorporation of performance indicators beyond structural mass.

It is in recognition of the fact that contemporary techniques are process based that references are introduced to biology, the live mixing of music, jazz and ecology in this issue; ecology here serve as generative engines to develop techniques, where the environment influences the outcome of the developmental process. For example, Ocean North use ecology as an organisational paradigm to precisely articulate the environment as a dynamically unfolding generative field. Their approach to design, emphasising the primacy of process, changes their approach to building. They seek to 'engender relational dynamics between material form, ambient conditions, social arrangements, habitational potential and the subject'. Cultural transformation is invigorated by the unforeseeable influences and accidents that result from this inclusive approach.

The transformation of contemporary conditions is brought about by exploiting contemporary techniques' potential to exploit new effects. Foreign Office Architects utilise the affective potential of architectural technique to develop alternatives. An example is using sequential, integrative addition to produce undetermined, increasingly more ambiguous spatial and programmatic effects that have the capacity to resonate at many different levels and scales within the architecture.

These effects are also produced at the microscopic level of material consistency. Johan Bettum describes the newly discovered potential of polymer composite materials (PCM) to produce novel aesthetic and spatial effects by varying their molecular consistency. These discoveries correspond to recent trends towards a temporally conditioned approach to surfaces with the consequent focus on materials and materials technologies. Bettum's PCMA projects demonstrate the meaningful and dynamic role that the articulation of surfaces can play in mass cultural transformation.

The effects of programmatic, spatial and material organisation question all previous limits on architecture, inside/outside and figure/ground, while provoking a new flexible system of open organisations. The actualisation of these organisations in projects should be understood in terms of their performative effects, which are measured by their capacity to produce new effects that transform culture. Various techniques, in combination with various material organisations, produce effects that demonstrate maximum cultural efficacy. Some of these effects are known and others are emergent.

In Preston Scott Cohen's entry for Eyebeam Atelier, an analogical reasoning format is used, which is intensified, so that as one moves through different levels it is only possible to apprehend one's relationship with that particular (scanned) space. Meanwhile, the

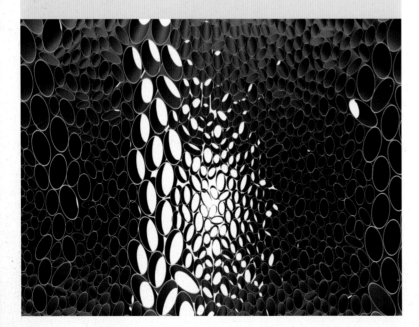

geometry of the toroids creates dramatically different spatio-temporal experiences from floor to floor. The resulting emergent structure helps to continue these variegated experiences at another scale, while systemically responding to the spatial articulation of the project. Here the form of the toroid produces a situation better than a conventional form creating an architectural paradox.

These new effects can also be created by recontextualising available techniques. Kolatan/Mac Donald Studio use lumping techniques to produce multiple new identities within programmatic and spatial configurations. The techniques are used as a recombinative logic to produce a series of new effects that provide for ranges of different programmatic protocols, appropriating and adapting the structures for the particular needs and desires of the inhabitants. These were built by recontextualising construction techniques used in the boatbuilding

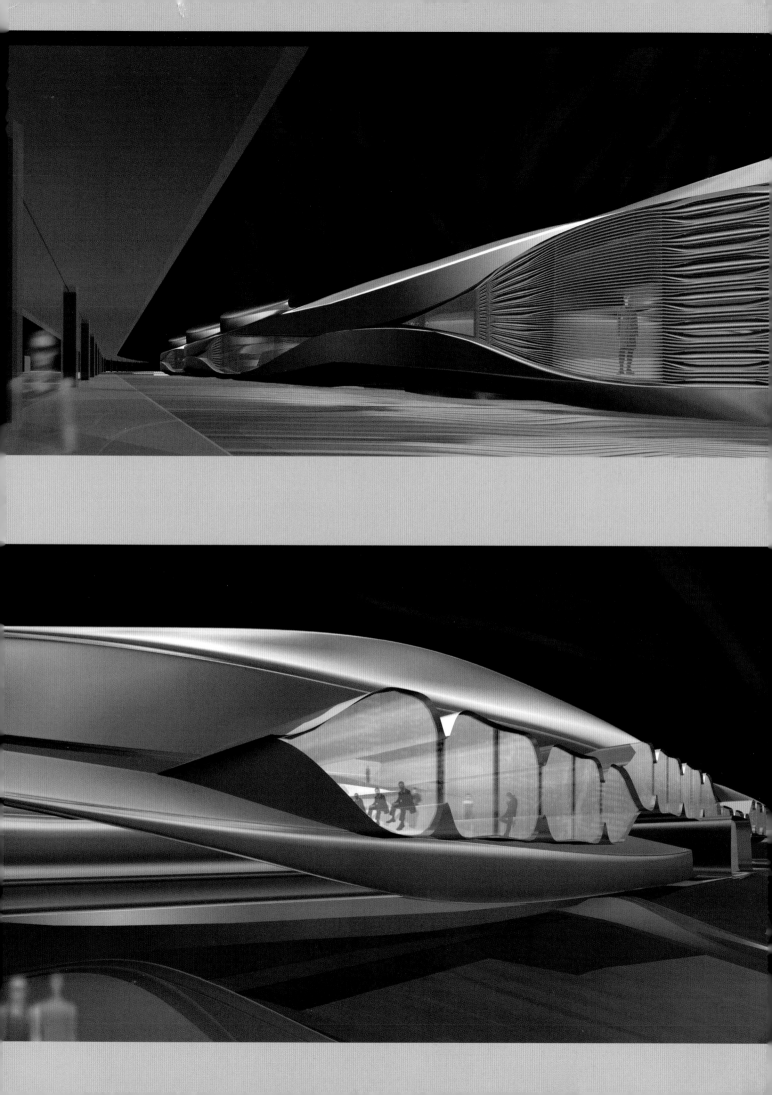

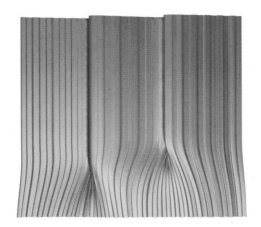

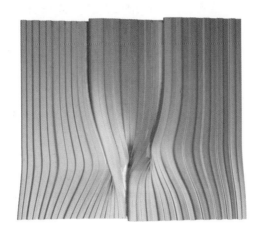

industry to vary and modulate the continuity of surface within the O/K Apartment renovations.

Contemporary techniques develop a new sensibility, one of geometric ambiguity, new composite forms and new ways of occupation in space. This spatiotemporal organisation guides the subject's experience with mixtures of different programmes that create new programmatic events, differentiated spaces and composite materials to organise experiences that affect the subject. Greg Lynn creates varying scales of spatial, material and ambient effects through the use of shredded vacuformed moulds engulfed in a Fabian painting. This organisation influences the behaviour patterns of the subject, resulting in the transformation of culture. This alters cultural development, and reformulates consequent effects to produce new techniques. The future of contemporary techniques resides in the production of a feedback loop capable of instantaneously testing the effects of their generative techniques.

Manufacturing and production techniques such as rapid prototyping, CNC milling, laser cutting, three-dimensional printing, mass customisation and flexible gel moulding should be understood as part of cultural proliferation. As culture adapts to the effects produced by contemporary techniques, the evolution of the cultural milieu is further influenced. Contemporary culture and contemporary techniques are developing simultaneously, with a profound effect on architectural production. Experimental architects are taking advantage of this simultaneity and the new techniques will eventually transform their static counterparts, currently used in the construction industry. ∆

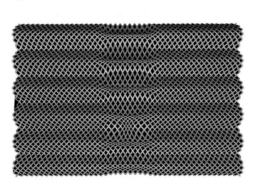

Right
Material research showing different porosities, which provide a range of gradient spatial and material effects. The threshold of the line is moved to a gradient so that opaque, translucent and transparent effects can occur in one surface in continuous variation. This re-articulates the intention to conflate the internal spatial effects while simultaneously producing aesthetic effects of various transparencies and lighting variation in one surface.

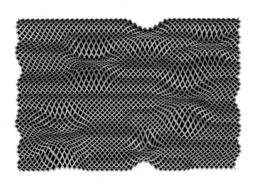

Deleuze and the Use of the Genetic Algorithm in Architecture

Manuel DeLanda exploits organisational processes in order to understand the possibilities contained within the computer programs known as 'genetic algorithms' – evolutionary simulations that replace normative design methods and aid in the breeding of new forms. This technique should be understood as a result of a complex feedback loop that exists between technology and culture. DeLanda uses the genetic algorithm to replace determinist notions of causality with non-linear, bottom-up, systemic process-driven techniques, which produce fertile spaces that are 'rich enough' for the evolutionary results to be exceptional, and sufficiently open-ended to make it impossible for the designer to consider all possible configurations in advance. These create emergent organisations of several variations instead of singular static objects.

The computer simulation of evolutionary processes is already a well-established technique for the study of biological dynamics. One can unleash within a digital environment a population of virtual plants or animals; and keep track of the way in which these creatures change as they mate and pass their virtual genetic materials to their offspring. The hard work lies in defining the relation between the virtual genes and the virtual bodily traits that they generate. The remaining tasks – keeping track of who mated with whom, assigning fitness values to each new form, determining how a gene spreads through a population over many generations – are performed automatically by computer programs known as 'genetic algorithms'. The study of the formal and functional properties of this type of software has now become a field in itself, quite separate from the applications in biological research which these simulations may have. In this essay I will not deal with the computer science aspects of genetic algorithms, or with their use in biology, but will focus instead on the applications which these techniques may have as aids in artistic design.

In a sense, evolutionary simulations replace design, since artists can use this software to breed new forms rather than to merely design them. However, as I argue below, there remains a part of the process in which deliberate design is still a crucial component. Since the software itself is relatively well known, and easily available, users may get the impression that breeding new forms has become a matter of routine. But it must also be noted that the space of possible designs in which the algorithm searches must be sufficiently rich for the evolutionary results to be truly exceptional. As an aid to design, these techniques would be rather useless if the designer could easily predict which forms would be bred.

Genetic algorithms will only serve as useful visualisation tools if virtual evolution can be used to explore a space in which it is impossible for the designer to consider all potential configurations in advance, and only if what results shocks, or at least surprises. In the task of designing fertile search spaces, certain philosophical ideas, traced to the work of Gilles Deleuze, play a crucial role. I would argue that the productive use of genetic algorithms necessitates the deployment of three philosophical forms of thought: populational, intensive and topological. Deleuze did not invent these but he brought them together for the first time, and made this the basis for a new concept of the genesis of form.

In order to utilise genetic algorithms, a particular field of art must first be used to solve the problem of representation in the final product in terms of the process that generated it. Then one must figure out how to represent this process itself as a well-defined sequence of operations. It is this sequence or, rather, the computer code that specifies it, that becomes the 'genetic material' of the object in question. This problem can be simplified through the use of computer-aided design, given that a CAD model of an architectural structure is already defined by a series of operations. For example, a round column is produced with the following directions:

1. Draw a line defining the profile of the column.
2. Rotate this line to yield a surface of revolution.
3. Perform a few 'Boolean subtractions' to carve out detail in the body of the column.

Some software packages store this sequence and may even make available the actual computer code corresponding to it. In this case, the code itself becomes the 'virtual DNA' of the column. (A similar procedure is followed to create each of the other structural and ornamental elements of a building.)

In order to understand the next step in the process, one must apprehend the basic tenets of 'population thinking'. This method of reasoning was employed in the 1930s by the biologists who synthesised the theories of Darwin and Mendel, thereby creating the modern version of evolutionary theory. This method of thinking can be encapsulated in the brief phrase, 'never think in terms of Adam and Eve, but always in terms of larger reproductive communities'. That is to say, although at any time an evolved form is realised in individual organisms, the population, not the individual, is the matrix for the production of form. Any given animal or plant architecture evolves slowly as genes propagate in a population – at different rates and at different times – so that a new form is slowly synthesised within the larger reproductive community.[1] The lesson for computer design is simply that once the relationship between the virtual genes and the virtual bodily traits of a CAD building has been worked out, as articulated above, an entire population – not just a 'couple' – of such buildings must be unleashed within the computer. The architect should add points at which spontaneous mutations may occur to the CAD sequence of operations. For example, in the case of a column, one should take: the relative proportions of the initial line; the centre of rotation; and the shape with which the Boolean subtraction is performed; and allow these mutant instructions to propagate and interact collectively over many generations.

To population thinking Deleuze adds another cognitive style, 'intensive thinking', which, in its present form, is derived from thermodynamics but has roots as far back as late medieval philosophy. The modern definition of an intensive quantity becomes clear when contrasted with its opposite, extensive quantity, which includes familiar magnitudes such as length, area and volume. These are defined as magnitudes that can be spatially subdivided, that is, a volume of water divided in half comprises two half volumes. The term 'intensive' on the other hand, refers to quantities like temperature, pressure or speed, which cannot be subdivided as such; that is, two halves of a volume of water at 90 degrees of temperature do not become two half volumes at 45 degrees of temperature, but rather two halves at the original 90 degrees. Although for Deleuze this lack of divisibility is important, he also stresses another feature of intensive quantities: a difference of intensity, which spontaneously tends to cancel itself out and, in the process, drives fluxes of matter and energy. In other words, differences of intensity are productive differences since they drive processes in which the diversity of actual forms is produced.[2] For example, the process of embryogenesis, which produces a human body out of a fertilised egg, is a process driven by differences of intensity (differences of chemical concentration, of density, of surface tension).

What does this mean for the architect? It means that unless one brings to a CAD model the intensive elements of structural engineering, basically distributions of stress, a virtual building will not evolve as a building. In other words, if the column I described above is not linked to the rest of the building, as a load-bearing element, by the third or fourth generation this column may be placed in such a way that it can no longer perform its function of carrying loads in compression. The only way to ensure that structural elements do not lose their function, and hence that the overall building does not lose viability as a stable structure, is to attempt to represent the distribution of stresses. One must show which types of concentrations, during the process that translates virtual genes into bodies, will endanger the structure's integrity. For example, in the case of real organisms if a developing embryo becomes structurally unviable it won't even reach reproductive age where it would be subject to the process of natural selection. It gets selected out prior to that. A similar process would have to be simulated in the computer to make sure that the products of virtual evolution are viable in terms of structural engineering prior to being selected by the designer in terms of their 'aesthetic fitness'.

Now, let us assume that these requirements have indeed been met, perhaps by an architect-hacker who takes existing software (a CAD package and a structural engineering package) in order to write a code that brings the two together. If the individual now sets out to use virtual evolution as a design tool, he or she may be disappointed by the fact that the only role left for a human is to be the judge of aesthetic fitness. The role of design has now been transformed into (some would say downgraded to) the equivalent of a racehorse breeder. There remains, clearly, an aesthetic component, but hardly the kind of creativity that one identifies with the development of a personal artistic style. Although today slogans about the 'death of the author' and attitudes against the 'romantic view of the genius' are in vogue, I expect this to be a fad and that questions of personal style will return to the spotlight. Will these future authors be content in the role of virtual form breeders? Not that the process, thus far, is routine in any

explores, had been exhausted.[3] This stands in sharp contrast to the incredible combinatorial productivity of natural forms like the thousands of original architectural 'designs' exhibited by vertebrate or insect bodies. Although biologists do not have a full explanation for this, one possible way of approaching the question is through the notion of a 'body plan'.

As vertebrates, the architecture of our bodies (which combines bones bearing loads in compression and muscles bearing them in tension) makes us part of the phylum Chordata. The term 'phylum' refers to a branch in the evolutionary tree (the first bifurcation after animal and plant 'kingdoms'), but it also carries the idea of a shared body plan. By this I mean an 'abstract vertebrate' which, if folded and curled in particular sequences during embryogenesis, yields, for example, an elephant that, when twisted and stretched in another sequence, yields a giraffe, and in yet other sequences of intensive operations yields snakes, eagles, sharks and humans. To put this differently, there are 'abstract vertebrate' design elements, such as the tetrapod limb, which may be realised in structures as different as the

As an aid to design, these techniques would be rather useless if the designer could easily predict which forms would be bred. Genetic algorithms will only serve as useful visualisation tools if virtual evolution can be used to explore a space in which it is impossible for the designer to consider all potential configurations in advance, and only if what results shocks, or at least surprises.

sense. After all, the original CAD model must be endowed with mutation points at just the right places. This involves design decisions and much creativity will still be needed to link ornamental and structural elements in just the right way. Nevertheless, this remains far from a design process by which one develops a unique style.

There is, however, another part of the process where stylistic questions are still crucial, although in a different sense than in ordinary design. Explaining this involves bringing in the third element in Deleuze's philosophy of the genesis of form: topological thinking. One way to introduce this style of thinking is to contrast the results artists have so far obtained with the genetic algorithm to those achieved by biological evolution. When one looks at current artistic results the most striking fact is that, once a few interesting forms have been generated, the evolutionary process seems to run out of possibilities. New forms do continue to emerge but they seem too close to the original ones, as if the space of possible designs, which the process

single digit limb of a horse, the wing of a bird or the hand with an opposing thumb of a human. Given that the proportion of each of these limbs, as well as the number and shape of digits, is variable, their common body plan cannot include any of these details. In other words, the form of the final product (an actual horse, bird or human) does have specific lengths, areas and volumes. But the body plan cannot possibly be defined in these terms and must be abstract enough to be compatible with many different combinations of these extensive quantities. Deleuze uses the term 'abstract diagram', or 'virtual multiplicity', to refer to entities akin to the vertebrate body plan, but his concept also includes the 'body plans' of nonorganic entities like clouds or mountains.[4]

What kind of theoretical resources do we need in order to analyse these abstract diagrams? In mathematics, those spaces in which terms like 'length' or 'area' constitute fundamental notions are called 'metric spaces'. The familiar Euclidean geometry is one example of this class, whereas non-Euclidean geometries, using curved instead of flat spaces, are also metric. On the other hand, there are geometries

Notes
1. 'First ... the forms do not preexist the population, they are more like statistical results. The more a population assumes divergent forms, the more its multiplicity divides into multiplicities of a different nature ... the more efficiently it distributes itself in the milieu, or divides up the milieu ... Second, simultaneously and under the same conditions ... degrees are no longer measured in terms of increasing perfection ... but in terms of differential relations and coefficients such as selection pressure, catalytic action, speed of propagation, rate of growth, evolution, mutation ... Darwinism's two fundamental contributions move in the direction of a science of multiplicities: the substitution of populations for types, and the substitution of rates or differential relations for degrees.' Gilles Deleuze and Felix Guattari, *A Thousand Plateaus*, University of Minnesota Press (Minneapolis), 1987, p 48.
2. 'Difference is not diversity. Diversity is given, but difference is that by which the given is given ... Difference is not phenomenon but the nuomenon closest to the phenomenon ... Every phenomenon refers to an inequality by which it is conditioned ... Everything which happens and everything which appears is correlated with orders of differences: differences of level, temperature, pressure, tension, potential, difference of intensity.' Gilles Deleuze, *Difference and Repetition*, Columbia University Press (New York), 1994, p 222.
3. See, for example, Stephen Todd and William Latham, *Evolutionary Art and Computers*, Academic Press (New York), 1992.
4. 'An abstract machine in itself is not physical or corporeal, any more than it is semiotic; it is diagrammatic (it knows nothing of the distinctions between the artificial and the natural either). It operates by matter, not by substance; by function, not by form ... The abstract machine is pure Matter-Function – a diagram independent of the forms and substances, expressions and contents it will distribute.' Deleuze and Guattari, op cit, p 141.

where these notions are not basic, since these geometries possess operations that do not preserve lengths or areas unchanged. Architects are familiar with at least one of these, projective geometry, as in the use of perspective projections. In this case, the operation 'to project' may extend or shrink lengths and areas so these cannot be basic notions. In turn, those properties which do remain fixed under projections may not be preserved under yet other forms of geometry, such as differential geometry or topology. The operations allowed in the latter, such as stretching without tearing, and folding without gluing, preserve only a set of abstract invariant properties. These topological invariants – such as the dimensionality of a space, or its connectivity – are precisely the elements we need in order to begin thinking about body plans or, more generally, abstract diagrams. It is clear that the kind of spatial structure defining a body plan cannot be metric, since embryological operations can produce a large variety of finished bodies, each with a different metric structure. Therefore body plans must be topological.

To return to the genetic algorithm: if evolved architectural structures are to enjoy the same degree of combinatorial productivity as biological ones, they must also begin with an adequate diagram, an 'abstract building', corresponding to the 'abstract vertebrate'. And it is at this point that design goes beyond mere breeding, with different artists designing different topological diagrams bearing their signature. The design process, however, will be quite different from the traditional one, which operates within metric spaces. It is indeed too early to say precisely what kind of design methodology will be necessary when one cannot use fixed lengths or even fixed proportions as aesthetic elements, but must rely instead on pure connectivities (and other topological invariants). But it is clear that without this the space of possibilities in which virtual evolution blindly searches will be too impoverished to be of any use. Thus, architects wishing to use the new tool of genetic algorithms must not only become hackers (so that they can create the code needed to bring extensive and intensive aspects together) but also be able 'to hack' biology, thermodynamics, mathematics and other areas of science to tap into the necessary resources. As fascinating as the idea of breeding buildings inside a computer may be, it is clear that mere digital technology without populational, intensive and topological thinking will never be enough. ∆

Emergent Structural
Morphology

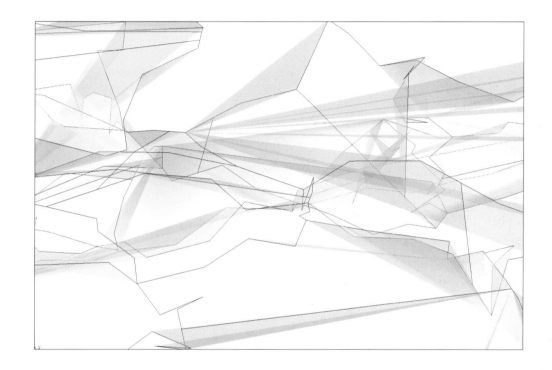

Peter Testa and **Devyn Weiser** develop 'theoretical frameworks and computational environments to relate computational thinking to the design process.' This transdisciplinary approach incorporates and adapts the very latest programming techniques from artificial intelligence, computational geometry, advanced structural engineering, manufacturing and material science, to establish a generative process. Their work brings about a synthesis between space-oriented and structure-oriented models, thereby creating self-regulatory patterns in which potentialities are regulated by the developing structure itself, through a process of interlocution within its individual components. The link between form and technique that is initiated within these discontinuous yet consanguine parts is mutable, and integrates non-linear combinations of digital and analogic sequences, innovative algorithims and intensive 'deep' computing techniques. These techniques result in the simulation of stochastic, evolutionary and environment based three-dimensional structures and surfaces.

The development of new material and building systems is closely linked with end-to-end process redesign that includes the inventive application of computational tools across design and manufacturing. Computation has become the engine of experimentation and research in architecture and structural engineering. Advances in computing technology have made the technique of simulation as crucial to design and engineering today as theory and experiment were in the past. The trend is evident in computational geometry, advanced structural engineering, material science and manufacturing. Many of these advances are related to the availability of high-performance computing and new software tools that enable high-speed generation and analysis of formal systems and structures, as well as new algorithms for searching, matching and aligning information. Powerful deep-computing techniques have been used to develop analytical tools, and still more powerful techniques will be required to fulfil the promise of emergent structural morphology. Deep computing implies the use of powerful machines running sophisticated software and using innovative algorithms to solve complex problems. But there is another more accessible approach to building *ad hoc* design machines which, when creatively applied, can vastly expand the design space and formal potentials of architecture and advanced structural design. This approach involves the modification and augmentation of existing and readily available tools and techniques.

In 1997, we founded the Emergent Design Group (EDG) at MIT to pioneer this new transdisciplinary design approach located at the intersection of architecture, artificial intelligence and material science. Our research develops theoretical frameworks and computational environments to relate computational thinking to the design process. Some of the themes we study are structural morphology, generative modelling of architectural form and building assemblies. While our projects find support in advanced computational techniques, they are also motivated by ongoing developments in material science. Today we are in the position not to simply specify material assemblies from catalogues, but to design materials adapted to specific aesthetic and tectonic objectives. This opens up radical new possibilities for architectural form but also demands new skills and insights from the designer.

Design Machines

Our research team has designed and implemented a series of tools that apply cutting-edge programming techniques from the domain of artificial intelligence and artificial life. The work is significant in inventing algorithms for environment-based, stochastic and evolutionary simulations of three-dimensional surfaces and structures.

The source code of our design machines, that is, the basic structure of how information works inside them, is a mutable link between form and technique that results from discontinuous yet related processes. We design our tools to deal with an interlocking or interaction of digital and analogic steps, as alternating processes instead of a linear series of steps that are all alike. To use computation creatively we have found that there must always be a generative process whereby the classes are created before they can be named. Evolutionary computation provides a readily available set of techniques and control models to generatively model the development of pattern, form and structure in architecture.

Various models of morphogenesis exist that use computer graphics to visualise the results of simulations. Przemyslaw Prusinkiewicz has succinctly characterised these models in two classes.[1] Space-oriented models capture the flow of information but have only limited capability to describe the structure embedded in the medium and its expansion, as growth is limited to the boundary. Structure-oriented models can simulate the expansion of the whole structure, but they do not inherently capture information flow through the medium. Our work represents a synthesis of both approaches with the goal of initiating self-regulatory patterns whereby growth is potentially controlled by the whole developing structure, using communication via the existing components of this structure.

Two of the software systems we have developed – Morphogenetic Surface Structure (MoSS) and Generative Form Modelling and Manufacturing (GENR8) – explore developmental mechanics and demonstrate aspects of the flow of control information during the development of multicellular structures. MoSS and GENR8 use programming languages to further architectural exploration, and assist in the development of a contemporary design approach that incorporates knowledge and awareness of structural forms and material qualities along with aesthetics and computational processes. Our tools enable the designer to envision structures, the potential in new forms and the possibilities of generating other forms, and to experiment with changeable forms through metamorphosis. As a result, spontaneity is a constant in this process as forms pass from one to the other.

Both tools are written in C++ as plug-ins to Alias|Wavefront Studio and Maya platforms. They are fully integrated with the Alias|Wavefront API and can be used in a manner similar to, and in conjunction with, the powerful modelling and simulation environment. The plug-in aspect implies the potential for these tools to be integrated with existing tools and conceptualised as part of a larger design process that includes simulation, evaluation and manufacturing.

Morphogenetic Surface Structures (MoSS)

MoSS uses a specialised implementation of 3D Lindenmayer systems (L-systems) that grow surfaces by applying rewrite rules to an axiom with an accompanying interpretation of movement and drawing in space. L-systems are based on recursive replacement of characters according to a set of grammar rules. The recursive replacement is limited by the number of generations specified for a run. In an L-system growth is controlled by a context-free or context-sensitive grammar. In MoSS the designer specifies the grammar and guides surface growth by defining shaping forces and boundary conditions. The environment in which a MoSS three-dimensional L-system operates ultimately decides the final geometry of a surface.

The interface includes control factors that establish grammar, limit generation and shape environment. For example, any number of attractors and repellors, points where growth is promoted or discouraged, can be added to create a complex growth environment with feedback. An attractor and repellor is defined as a point in 3D space. Around this point, movement and drawing are warped to force movement closer to the attractor or further from the repellor. The amount of warping depends on distance and force. This force is parameterised for the user to set. Attractors and repellors significantly alter the generated surface from its specification in axiom and production-rule terms. They can be used to represent various forces in the environment.

One example of a structural system that has emerged from the MoSS research programme is the free-form honeycomb truss. In this system, vertices of generated surfaces are joined to form an adaptive three-dimensional cellular structure. The structures may be produced with sheet materials or as a matrix to be filled with structural foam. We are exploring a cellular membrane, using advanced composite materials in which cell geometry, size, wall thickness and depth are simultaneously varied in response to stress and various loading conditions. The longer term goal is to develop tools for generating cellular structures and structural membranes. These constructs should exhibit local or microscopic behaviour in length and time scales related to their thickness, and macroscopic behaviour in length and time scales related to growth and movement perpendicular to their surface.

Generative Form Modelling and Manufacturing (GENR8)

In an effort to create a bridge between local and global simulation of cellular structures, we implemented GENR8, a software system for emergent simulations that uses Map L-systems. Map L-systems extend the expressive power of L-systems beyond branching structures to graphs with cycles – called maps – that represent cellular layers. GENR8 is a Map L-system with geometric interpretation that operates first by establishing the neighbourhood relations between the cells, then assigning geometric parameters to the resulting graph. Grammar-based rules specify a model's topology, which sequentially determines its geometry. GENR8 combines 3D Map L-systems, which are extended to an abstract physical environment, with Grammatical Evolution. An innovative aspect of this tool is that it fuses expressively powerful languages for simulating growth with evolutionary search.

GENR8 addresses key issues arising from exploiting evolutionary adaptation within an interactive design tool. Evolutionary Algorithms (EAs) typically adapt 'off line' but GENR8 is designed to accommodate iterative control exchange between user and tool during on-line evolutionary adaptation. It allows users to interrupt, intervene and then resume an EA tool. In addition to user-based interactive design evaluation it also offers the option of computationalised multicriteria evaluation to enable wider searches in shorter time spans. Constructing grammars by hand is tedious and difficult. To generate and evaluate the universe of possible grammars, we use Grammatical Evolution. GENR8 has two mapping processes, one that maps a genome to a grammar and another that interprets the grammar and constructs a surface (phenotype).

GENR8 has a powerful simulation environment that significantly influences growth. In the current instance, there are three types of forces: attractors, repellors and gravity. As in MoSS, attractors and repellors can be used to direct growth. The user situates them in space and their effect depends on the relative location of the surface being modelled. The user may also draw arbitrary surfaces and volumes that act as boundaries.

A key issue for EAs is the fitness evaluation. GENR8 allows the user to express preferences by setting the parameters of the fitness function. Five independent fitness criteria are implemented: size, smoothness, soft boundaries, subdivisions and symmetry. The different (independent) parameters can be used to express multilevel, nonlinear and possibly conflicting design criteria. Similarly, the weight and parameters of any criterion can be changed at any time during a run. The fitness function has several parameters (rewarding different features of the surface) and modifying these will alter the ranking of individuals. The user can guide evolution by setting fitness values by hand. The user

Note
1. Przemyslaw Prusinkiewicz, 'Visual models of morphogenesis' in C Langton (ed), *Artificial Life*, MIT Press (Cambridge MA), pp 61–74.

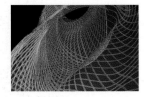

can also indirectly affect fitness by changing an individual and inserting those copies into the population. It is also possible to insert another population (previously saved to a file) into the existing population. This enables the user to insert new formants in a controlled way.

Looking further ahead, there is a need to instantiate growth models with the capability to combine the atomic structure and mechanical properties of materials, and the macro behaviour of the structure as a whole operating in a dynamic environment. This would lead to different control models for different materials, and different grammars for the larger structure related to specific material properties. In this way tunable factors in the materials may be adapted through mutualist feedback with the emergent structural morphology as a whole. For example, atomistic simulation of materials using force-field parameters or methods based on high-capacity molecular dynamics may allow us to evolve highly tuned and sophisticated material forms and three-dimensional structures on all scales.

Carbon Tower Prototype

To further develop and apply our research in emergent structural morphology we have founded the Hyperarchitecture Research Center (HYPR) in the Department of Civil and Environmental Engineering at MIT. A primary research platform for this new centre is focused on developing an innovative tensile building system using advanced composite materials. We are currently developing a prototype of a 40–60-storey high-rise and have received a preliminary patent. All the developments described in the preceding EDG projects, from computational tools to materials and manufacturing and the goal of fusing surface and structure, are being incorporated in this new project.

The structures of the future require minimum materials and maximum performance. Advanced composite materials, primarily developed in aerospace, defence and other industries, are finding more applications in civil engineering and they emerge as attractive future construction materials. Structures made of these materials enjoy a host of benefits because they are stiff, strong, light and formable. However, their use in buildings and other structures is currently limited because of inherent design requirements.

In our system, compressive loads are carried by an array of vertical columns and cores, constructed on site using high-strength steel-reinforced concrete and composite reinforcing. In contrast to the traditional 'bottom-up' construction schemes, our approach is to construct the compression members (the cores) first, and then build the structural skeleton from the top to the bottom. A composite mesh formed of continuous pultruded sections is hung from this compressive structure. Operating in concert with Kevlar cables, this exterior meshwork supports the floor slabs. These are laminated resin slabs with a composite mesh continuous with the exterior tensile envelope. All connections between elements are made using high-strength adhesives. The resulting hybrid structure combines a flexible building envelope with a rigid core, yielding a structure that is earthquake resistant. The open interior plan is combined with a variable section as the floors are independent of the constrictions of frame and curtain-wall construction.

A key concept in this system is the use of a tensile mesh or woven structure suspended from the compressive cores. We are developing new pultrusion and robotic technology to weave the structural envelope on site. In the new enclosure system, transparent resins and silicone membranes allow for a spectral and smooth exchange from opaque, reflective, translucent to transparent, without sacrificing the structural properties of the enclosure. The layering of exterior skins can be developed as a series of plenums, supporting natural ventilation. In order to better design the system, we are coding different generative structural design and analysis tools. For example, we designed a tool to generate woven meshes called WEAVER. It allows the user to explore patterns that can either be used to generate the building morphology or be applied to a shape established by other parameters.

We address the potential integration of sensors and active materials within this structural system and material assemblies. The feedback is necessary as a means of monitoring the integrity of components during the construction process. Damage and failure in composite materials are exceedingly difficult to detect. Embedded sensors can also serve as an active component throughout the life of the structure, allowing for real-time adaptation to dynamic loading conditions and differential movements between highly stable composite materials and other material systems used in construction.

Application Oriented Basic Research

The digital revolution combined with the rapid development of new materials and prototyping technology has fundamentally changed the way buildings are designed and constructed. New tools and techniques are required to capture the emergent relations among evolving material properties, structural morphology, manufacturing technology and architectural form. Our work is foundational to this next step in design, which integrates the propensity of materials and manufacturing processes within generative computing. ∆

Above
WEAVER uses a grammar capable of describing and generating woven strands to a user-defined surface. The resulting weaves can be complex, and depend on both the description of the weave pattern and the topology of the surface on which the weave is applied. MEL script for Alias|Wavefront Maya.

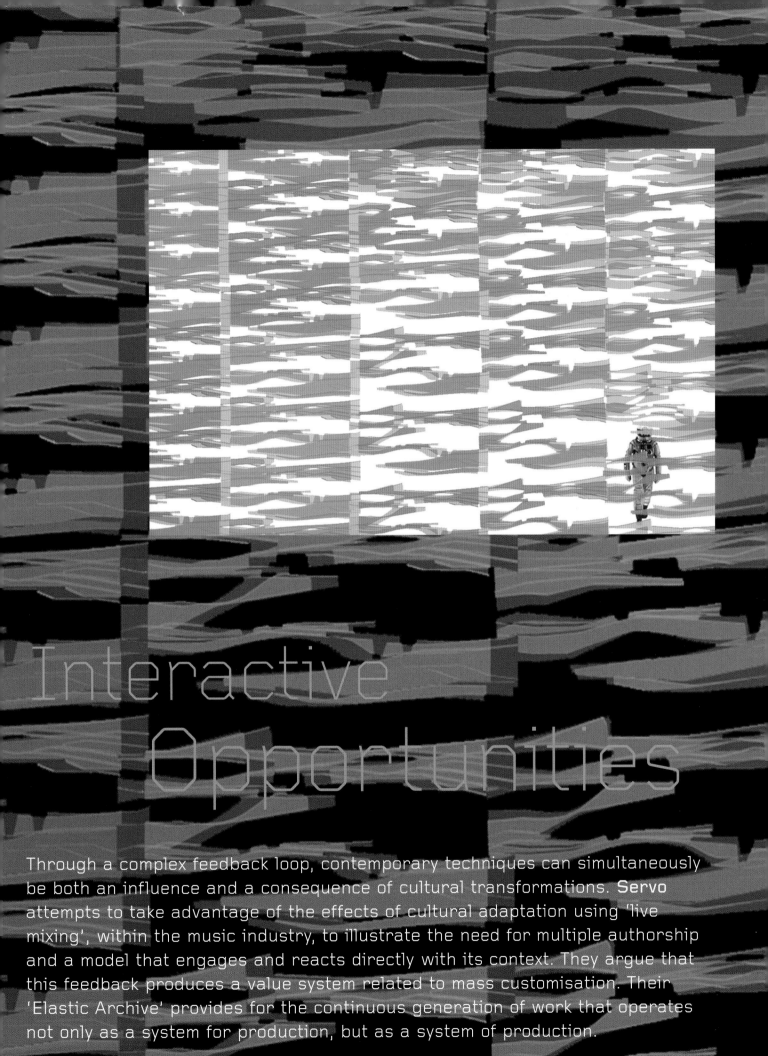

Interactive
Opportunities

Through a complex feedback loop, contemporary techniques can simultaneously be both an influence and a consequence of cultural transformations. Servo attempts to take advantage of the effects of cultural adaptation using 'live mixing', within the music industry, to illustrate the need for multiple authorship and a model that engages and reacts directly with its context. They argue that this feedback produces a value system related to mass customisation. Their 'Elastic Archive' provides for the continuous generation of work that operates not only as a system for production, but as a system of production.

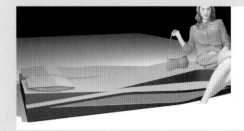

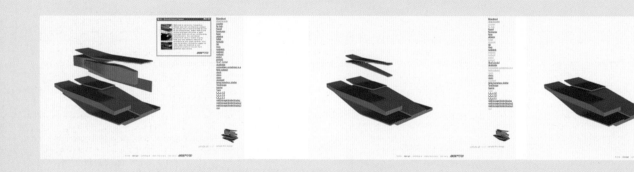

Previous page
Elevational study of the
'cloudcurtain'.

Top and opposite top
The Nurbwall and Nurbrests
are case studies within the
nurbline which can be
designed and manipulated at
the servoline_1 website. The
Nurbwall provides an
interlocking shelving system
on rails or wheels suitable for
library stacks, archives or
other storage and display
applications. It is constrained
for manufacture in aluminium,
wood or fibreglass. It has
opportunities to be appropriated
and misappropriated as an
interior partitioning system
for various space-planning
conditions, simultaneously
providing potential exhibition
surfaces for private or
commercial display. The
Nurbrest functions as a
flexible rest system which
generates hybrid conditions
between bench, couch and bed
allowing one's body to occupy
the prototype in both
horizontal and vertical
conditions. The designs
equally require multiple
authors to interact in different
envelopes of use.

Servo motors translate digital code into machinic processes. They behave principally as enablers which allow two distinct languages to converse and interact. For Servo, this has been the primary way in which we have constructed and considered the practice of our collaborative. Notions of collaboration are pervasive in architectural culture from Bunschaft with Nogouchi, to more explicit interactions like the Independent Group, Archigram, Team 10 or OMA. Servo positions itself as a collaborative that is constructed through contemporary modes of communication and lifestyle. We are four people, each inhabiting a geographically different urban space – spanning one ocean, two continents and three countries. Much of our work is concerned with, and informed by, the ways in which we interact and how opportunities, or perhaps cartels, can be constructed through such a dispersed notion of office, production and conversation. As an architecture and design practice, Servo has explored the possibilities of a conversational model that engages and samples from other disciplines, thinkers and audiences.

Servo continuously generates work, not tying it to specific commissions or venues. The work is recontextualised and adapted by shuffling and moving it between the respective members of the group through a filter called an 'elastic archive'. This is a dynamic storage mechanism in the form of project lines: hard drives, ftp sites, and organisational diagrams which are always growing, sampling new material and being resituated. The nature of this 'archive' throws into question conventional distinctions between design, display and storage, merging the practices and technologies of each into an interactive design process. Servo has consequently investigated two parallel forms of browsing and sorting. First, through digital interface design and its presentation and organisation in physical spaces: for instance, converting gallery space into labs, or display systems into infrastructure for buildings or communication. Second, through seeking to alter protocols of design, in the digital realm, in a way that explicitly affects the manufacturing of a physical object. This has raised issues of use and scale in which each of Servo's three 'project lines' examines modularity as an informatic entity, allowing organisational systems to operate at multiple scales from a hand-held toy to an urban proposition. ᔉ

Below left

The Cloudcurtain is the largest scale application in the Cloudline: in part a response to the recent replacement of curtain walls on modern skyscrapers converted from commercial to residential use, and in part a response to an emerging infiltration of signage, light infrastructure and provisional programmes into conventional building skins. The Cloudcurtain provides for a variety of potential uses. It is a snap-on curtain wall system that utilises a pattern of numeric codes, based on drawings, to cut conduits into the surface of a transparent plastic skin. By reversing conventions of mechanical and electrical distribution through the core of the building, the Cloudcurtain employs the skin itself as a field for conduits, thus allowing for greater accessibility and flexibility as companies upgrade and rewire buildings. It is an architecture which houses and responds to technological needs while simultaneously exhibiting the technology, which constructs itself as a spectacle.

Below right

The Cloudline is an examination of ways in which a computer numerically controlled (CNC) mill can shift the material properties of plastic and utilise patterning as a vehicle for distributing electrical infrastructure and partially programming space. Picking up on the fact that CNC mills can shift 2D information (drawings) into 3D cuts by simply adding Z coordinate information to a drawing, and that they are generally used to remove material, the cloud pattern examines techniques in which pocket cutting can shift the character of plastic and the set of possibilities for a wall. A set of 2D closed curves, forming a granular wood-like pattern are reinterpreted and given a Z dimension embedding a pattern of pockets into plastic panels. Clear plastic, an otherwise mute material, one without a structural direction and one which attempts to disappear, takes on qualities of grain and texture in addition to containing varying qualities of translucency and transparency as a result of the embedded pattern. The technique affords two distinct possibilities. First, because the pattern is 2D and the CNC mill is where Z dimensions are set, it can be broken into modules of information, repeated and scaled up or down. This informatic module then is independent of standard material sizes.

Second, the space generated in the cavity of the wall can be exploited for a host of purposes, from the distribution of electronic infrastructure at one scale, to the distribution of small building programmes at another.

Opposite bottom

The servoline_1 website modelling interface designed by *Servo* for the Nordic netart foundation is an exploration of the limits to which architectural design, through contemporary manufacturing and digital coding techniques, can involve multiple authors. The Interface User combines and resituates curves. Servo designs the curve set delimiting the extent and parameter of the curves and ensures that curve assemblies are manufacturable. The Programmer decodes the assembly as java script and recodes it as machine code where, finally, the Manufacturer filters the code through Servo motors and into the Interface User's specified material.

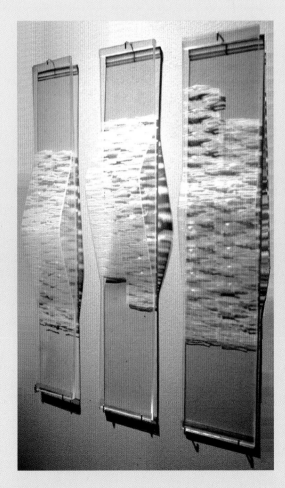

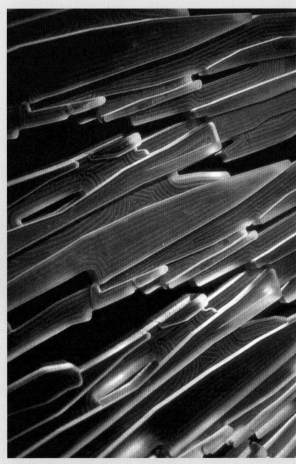

Toroidal
Architecture

'Toroidal Architecture' is the manifestation of **Preston Scott Cohen's** own geometric techniques, which produce effects at the scale of programme, space, material and structure. Programme is literally moved from the functionalist core to the perimeter, while the spatial sequence is intensified through the geometry of the toroids. The resulting emergent structure negotiates these toroids and provides another scale of obstacles that adapt to different spatial circumstances. This produces a 'perverse functionality', in which the form performs its function even better than if it were to perform normally.

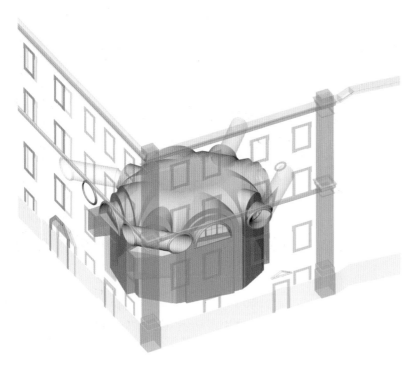

It has been suggested that the Torus House conjures up Mies van der Rohe's horizontal symmetries and free-plan interiors. The living space extends into the panoramic landscape through a glass curtain wall. More specifically, the Torus House appears to be comparable to Mies's Tugendhat House where horizontal spaces are stacked one on top of the other. Yet, the plan of the Torus House does not project into the landscape in the manner that Mies's Concrete Country House does, for example. The Torus House is compact. Its parts are contiguous along their lengths, not their ends. And, unlike Tugendhat, the Torus House has outdoor spaces above and below the interior that are connected to each other.

Reference to the torus requires that the main space of the house remains undivided, with the effect of displacing all of the compartmentalised spaces. In this sense, the Torus House can be more aptly compared to Mies's late work, that is, to the clear-span projects. The division between the emptiness of the living space and the dense perimeter of rooms is analogous to the pavilion vs podium dichotomy of Mies. But, in the Torus House, the separation is in the plan while in Mies's model it occurs in section. The fundamental difference, however, is that while Mies's vertical segregation is based on an *a priori* principle of space, the toroidal displacement of programme to the perimeter is based on a concept of surface.

Compare the cores of the two spatial paradigms, and their differences immediately come to the fore. Strictly functional and formally superfluous, the Miesian core is inessential to the open-space paradigm which it could do well without. This becomes most evident in the early 1953 version of Crown Hall which is without intrusive cores. Whereas the core in Mies is the result of the antithetical dualism between functional and aesthetic space, the core of the torus is indivisible from the whole; it is the essential defining feature of the torus.

Perverse Functionality

The clarity of Mies's dualism was reinforced by the separation and hierarchical distribution of functions. In contrast, the unity of the torus is architecturally paradoxical; though the space at its centre is literally exterior, it is nevertheless circumscribed as a territory within. At once outside and inside, it is difficult to make it functional. In the Torus House the core espouses not just any functionality, but rather a perverse functionality: the condition in which something performs its function even better than it would had it been able to perform normally. This idea comes from natural philosophers of the 17th century who were fascinated by rarities, monsters and the like: forms derived through processes of adaptation under difficult circumstances. Such forms were evidence of nature's ingenuity in overcoming difficult odds. At the Torus

House, the peculiar division and equivocation of space introduced by the toroidal paradox produces an entry sequence even more fitting to the client, a landscape painter who regularly paints and entertains on his roof, than the usual threshold would. One ascends a stair that leads from the ground floor carport directly to the roof. This vertical sequence replaces what is occasionally experienced as a somewhat disconcerting, horizontal scenario – the summertime guests' voyeuristic passage through an empty house on the way to a party in the backyard. In this case the front door is below the house, the backyard is on top and guests bypass the interior while passing through it.

The 17th century did not generally yield examples of perverse functionality in architecture. But today, through the lens of an anachronistic hypothesis, the Baroque sacristy of San Carlo ai Catinari in Rome appears to be an exception. The problem at the sacristy was the demand for an embrasure to be located on the interior in a position that would normally require it to pierce through an exterior corner pilaster. Such a result was censured, in advance, by classical codes of decorum. Today, by means of a geometric technique, the embrasure can be rotated in a process that produces the final anomalous form: a tubular void piercing the corner of the building. This form would also have been forbidden had it not been inconspicuous. Fortuitously, the geometric procedure of rotation sets into motion the production of patterns and congruencies among the windows that altogether disguise the anomalous tubular episode as a regular one. The imperative to conceal the exceptional condition produced a rare intertwining of elements and systems of order in the classical architectural canon that arguably evolved the canon to a higher level. Furthermore, the rotated tubular embrasure emits light that appears more 'supernatural' than it would if it came from a normal embrasure. Given that the creation of a mysterious light effect was a primary function of the deep embrasures in Baroque Rome, the rotated tubular void performs better than the norm. Though it did not elicit curiosity during its time (it was neither spectacular nor conspicuous enough for the era of curiosity and wonder), by means of projective geometry, using today's tools of modelling, the sacristy becomes a demonstrable case of perverse functionality.

Eyebeam Atelier's Museum of Art and Technology in New York demands a duality, one that combines exhibition and education facilities, at a scale that precludes the development of a single paradoxical surface or lineament. The multiplication, stacking and alternation of toroids evinces a congruent duality between mutually exclusive spaces of equal weight. Ascending and descending sequences of escalators and spaces run in tandem with one another. This model provides a coherent circuitous promenade that, unlike Wright's Guggenheim, deploys the normal horizontal floor plates that are commonly necessary for museum programmes.

Inversive Structures

For Eyebeam, it is the structural system that is most emphatically paradoxical. Tensegrity, a dual force-field of separate compression members held apart by cords in continuous tension, is at once coherent and episodic. How then is this structure implicated in the toroidal spatial discourse? It pierces as well as supports the multiple toroidal surfaces.

In contrast, the Goodman House is, once again, a single volume that is as undivided as possible. The surface of the volume contains, as well as passes through, the 19th-century timber structural frame that supports it. The outer surface of the volume extends

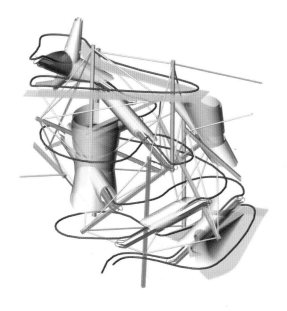

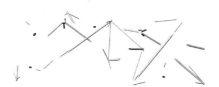

into a hollow core that traverses the width of the house. The house turns outside in. On the exterior, the core is a wind chamber. From inside the house, the core appears to be a giant inhabitable structural beam that occupies, as well as justifies (after the fact), an anomalous structural bay that was added to the original structure in the early 20th century. The interior and exterior of the house are two mutually exclusive, interlocked spaces.

Perhaps the most explicit hint of inversion that pertains to structure in Mies is in his 'Museum for a Small City'. In order to accommodate a clearing in the plan, the structure inverts along a single roof plane from inside to outside and from below to above. A grid of columns supports the building's roof from below. At the auditorium, suspended structural trusses support the roof from above. Though it responds to a functional and spatial demand, the premise of the inversion remains structural. Nevertheless, it is compelling to recognise that during the brief transition between the early and late Mies, between his European and American periods, there is a singular hybrid project that yields an analogue to the toroidal spatial thesis. ⌂

Top
Eyebeam Atelier, loop diagram for the proposed Museum of Art and Technology, New York.

Middle
Tensegrity/space diagrams for the Museum of Art and Technology.

Bottom and opposite
The floors of the Museum of Art and Technology are like horizontal cutting planes or scans of tensegrity. Moving a floor up or down – even slightly – and recutting it results in a radically different plan.

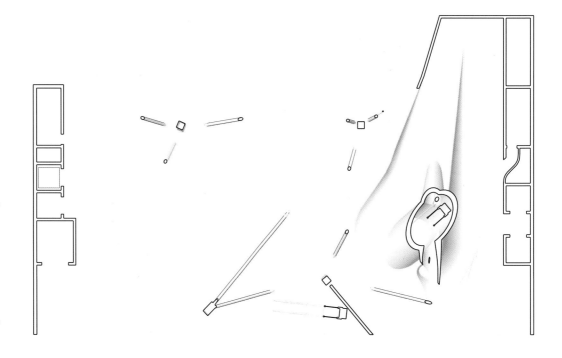

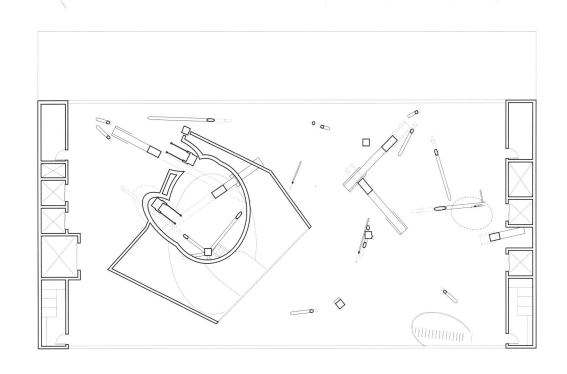

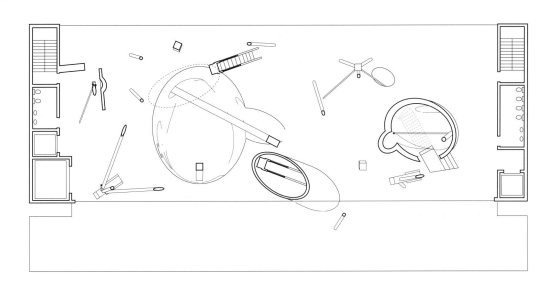

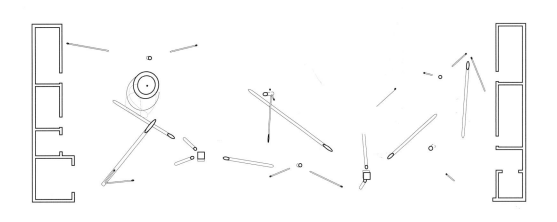

This page and opposite
Eyebeam Atelier, interior
images and section for the
proposed Musuem of Art
and Technology, New York.
The computer enhances the
capacity to introduce
complexity, ie proportionality,
into architecture. Whereas
proportion designates a
primary arithmetical system,
proportionality designates
a system of systems or
analogues. The predisposition
of architecture towards
analogical reasoning and
formatting is intensified
by the digital medium.

Gottfried Semper:
Stereotomy, Biology and Geometry

Bernard Cache posits that the environment influences the outcome of the developmental process through a complex feedback loop. He is mindful of the fact that digital-aided techniques are founded on two historically disconnected layers of geometry – antique Euclidian geometry and Renaissance perspectival geometry. Here he refers to Gottfried Semper in a biologic analogy that describes possibilities for the generation of any species through varying the proportions of its 'Urtier'. Cache uses this analogue to assert the need within architecture to develop existing techniques of projective geometry.

Will inflection turn out to be fluctuation or tendency? This question keeps on puzzling us at Objectile. As a digital-design company based in Paris, we are only too conscious of the fact that computers and 3D software give anyone the possibility of pulling passing points and drawing Nurb surfaces, which with appropriate funding might conceivably become buildings one day. With this in mind, Objectile pursues two separate but parallel lines of research. On the one hand, we actually intensify the dangers by developing software tools that are capable of making free-shape buildings affordable for any small architectural practice - just as word-processors and home printers gives anyone the means to publish glossy documents; while on the other hand, we have absolutely no faith in 'information', as such, and we become extremely critical when we hear about 'digital technologies' as something 'brand new'. We regard novelty as a marketing strategy for big companies in this field, which gives them the illusion of being self generated 'by teams of young cool guys'. By taking even a quick look at Richard Feynmann's lecture on computation, it is apparent just how deeply rooted in the past these new technologies are. Computing has a history, both hardware and software. Focusing on the latter, we would go so far as to affirm that Euclid's Elements were the first program ever written - still running bugfree behind any CAM package. A second layer being provided by projective geometry, which happened to have been created by architects such as Brunelleschi, Philibert De L'Orme and Desargues. Due to the intricacies of the history of projective geometry, we are not sure that architecture has drawn all the consequences of this additional layer in geometry. In the end, wouldn't computing have the potential of providing us with a vital way of reconnecting architecture to its own history?

Our point of departure today is referred to mathematically as a double point, in this case signified by two statues Gottfried Semper placed on top of the Museum of Natural History in Vienna. They represent the naturalist Georges Cuvier and Alexander von Humboldt, a German disciple of the zoologist Geoffroy Saint-Hilaire. The fact that Semper did not include a single biologist at the summit of his attempt to represent the discipline of science emphasises an absence that is further manifested within his treatise, *Der Stil*. Moreover, his placing of a statue of a disciple of Geoffroy Saint-Hilaire betrays an ambivalence that can, perhaps, also be noted in *Der Stil*.

The four technical arts discussed in the treatise are not given equal amounts of space. Semper's emphasis on textiles is well known as is Cuvier's predilection for molluscs, but I was previously unaware of the weakness of the section on stereotomy. It is not only the relatively few pages dedicated to this discipline, but the relative sparseness of its coverage compared with the amount of space devoted to tectonics in stone. It is even more surprising that Semper asserts that the history of architecture proves the victory of the vault over the tectonic frame (generally known as stereotomy) but fails to elaborate further on this theme. The absence of any significant discussion of stereotomy is particularly perplexing in light of the fact that he lived and studied in France, where the discipline was an architectural speciality. One wonders how such a learned scholar as Semper could write about stereotomy without even mentioning Philibert de L'Orme or Desargues. Did this reflect his acknowledgement of the decline of the French building tradition? Was his omission related to the controversy over Soufflot's Sainte-Geneviève church, where the old geometrical approach was to be supplanted by a physical approach in terms of stability and strength of materials? Or did he simply reject a tradition that was no longer able to cope with the problems of the day?

None of these can explain why Semper failed to mention that most Semperian piece of architecture: the exquisite stone interlacings of the rood screen within Saint-Etienne du Mont, just metres away from Sainte-Geneviève. Indeed, no other piece of architecture embodies so completely the architectural motif of the knot, and the theoretical concept of transposition from textile to stone. Could it be that what really hindered Semper was the fact that Philibert de L'Orme was not only the presumed architect of the rood screen – in addition to many other Semperian pieces of architecture such as the interlaced ribs of the vaults of the Château d'Anet – but was also responsible for the advent of projective geometry, which happened to be Geoffroy Saint-Hilaire' conceptual background? One might argue that Semper could easily have ignored projective geometry, and the fact that this particular type of geometry provided the building blocks of Saint-Hilaire's biology. But then we are reminded that Semper actually studied mathematics with Carl Friedrich Gauss himself, the man referred to as 'the prince of mathematics', who was the first to accept the implications of negating Euclid's fifth postulate and thereby inaugurated 'non-Euclidean geometry'.

So, we will risk the hypothesis that Semper was capable of fully understanding projective geometry, but chose to ignore it because it implied a refounding of geometry that was not yet fully explored within the field of mathematics, namely by Felix Klein in his Erlanger Programm in 1872. Until this refounding was achieved,

Opposite
Objectile, cladding detail of the Semper Pavilion, which was constructed and shown at the Archilab Exhibition, Orléans 1999 and Batimat, Paris, 1999.

geometry was bound to remain neoclassic. We will go so far as to suggest that Semper – whose first serious job called for him to re-establish a reading of Greek architecture by proof of colour – was unable to conduct the same operation on shape. Colour and surface, semantically close as Aristotle reminds us (*chroia* and *chroma*), testified to a pre-Euclidean polychrome geometry where colour and surface remained inextricably linked.

In the following paragraphs we will attempt to support this (admittedly venturous) hypothesis. First, it is necessary to demonstrate that projective geometry was an influential part of Geoffroy Saint-Hilaire's background – so much so that it could not be ignored by anyone with a triple interest in architecture, biology and mathematics. We then have to show how projective geometry implies a reading of geometry that is not neoclassical, and that would have been instrumental in assisting Semper to apply to shape the task he had already begun with colour and to adequately write his piece on stereotomy.

Let us start with biology. What was the core of Cuvier and Geoffroy Saint-Hilaire's argument that impassioned even Goethe and Balzac? Let us remember that the two biologists were good friends, and worked together on the vertebrates to corroborate Saint-Hilaire's view that a single structural plan informed the whole of this animal embranchment. Since 1796, he had been persuaded by Vicq d'Azir that there was such a plan for all animals. But he proceeded progressively, starting with mammals, then moving on to tetrapods. In 1807–8, in an essay on fish, he expanded this single plan to include all the vertebrates. At this point, Cuvier still agreed with Saint-Hilaire.

But in 1812, Cuvier announced his own thesis which classified animals according to four embranchments: the vertebrates, the molluscs, the articulated and the radials. He had a fixist view of biology, in which every single part is precisely fitted to its environment so that there is only one way each part can be connected to the entire organism. Lest I seem to be digressing too far from architecture let us remember Cuvier's famous sentence, which was adopted as a founding principle of Functionalist architecture: 'Give me any single piece of an animal and I will draw you the whole body.' According to this well-ordered view of nature, each embranchment has its own organisation and there can be no other way of connecting the parts.

Until 1820, Cuvier and Saint-Hilaire lived in Paris and worked cooperatively together at the Museum of Natural History. It was in 1814, as Hervé Le Guayader notes, that Savigny, who had been in Egypt with Saint-Hilaire during the Napoleonic campaign, studied the comparative anatomy of the insect's mouth and the

entomologist Pierre Latreille applied the principle of unity of composition to all articulated animals – insects, shellfish, arachnids, etc. Until 1820 relations between the two men remained excellent because Saint-Hilaire and his followers did not challenge Cuvier's four embranchments. But in that year Saint-Hilaire suggested that the vertebrates and insects shared a unity of plan. Criticism of Cuvier increased – even more so when Saint-Hilaire relied on works by Laurencet and Meyrand to extend his theory of unity of composition to molluscs. Laurencet and Meyrand had argued that the layout of a cephalopod's organs was analogous to that of the vertebrates because of a folding operation that was already implied by the etymology of the word cephalo-pode. According to this theory, three of Cuvier's four embranchments would be unified, something that Cuvier could not accept.

Let us first examine the breakdown of the division between the vertebrates and insects. It is important to realise that the relationship between these two embranchments is far from obvious since each of them has a thoroughly different relation to the ground. A vertebrate's digestive organs face it and are located underneath the vertebral column which houses the nervous system. This structure is clearly different to an insect's whose mouth is towards the ground, but whose digestive system remains in an inverted position facing the sky while the spinal cord lies underneath the body. A reader of *Der Stil* would immediately be reminded of the vectorial organisation evoked by Semper when he compares the composition of biological vectors in various species – that is, vectors of growth and movement versus the vector of gravity. Let us note the common use of vectorial diagrams by both Saint-Hilaire and Semper. But the French biologist goes further than the German architect, making use of a torsion operation to explain how insects maintain their bellies upwards and their backs downwards. This becomes particularly interesting when, for instance, he speaks of fish swimming upside down.

Nevertheless, the fact remains that Saint-Hilaire committed a series of errors when he went so far as to assert that 'each animal lives either inside or outside its spine', assimilating the carapace of insects with vertebrates hosting the spinal cord. Eventually, he would even compare the legs of shellfish to vertebrates ribs. It was therefore not difficult for Cuvier to take advantage of these errors in his attempt to invalidate the bulk of Saint-Hilaire's thought. As a result, he emerged as the winner in the final confrontation that took place in 1830 – the very time when Semper was accustomed to making long visits to the Jardins des Plantes. It is interesting to note that Cuvier maintained his advantage until 1996 when *Nature*, a prominent scientific journal, published an article by EM de

Robertis and Y Sassai entitled 'A common plan for dorso-ventral patterning in Bilateria'. The article's first sentence reads: 'Functional studies seem now to confirm, as first suggested by E Geoffroy Saint-Hilaire in 1822, that there was an inversion of the dorso-ventral axis during animal evolution.' Modern biology has found genes which code the orientation of organs backward and forward, as well as downward and upward, whose mutations explain how such a torsion was possible. As a result, the most plausible hypothesis now is that insects and vertebrates had a common ancestor from which they bifurcated some 540 millions years ago.

But let us now return to the beginning of the 19th century and focus on the geometrical concepts used by Saint-Hilaire. We have emphasised that the key concept was inversion, which also happens to be a key transformative principle within projective geometry. An inversion of power 'k', relative to a pole O, is the transformation which associates to a point M the point M1 such as OM*OM1 = k. One immediately sees that:

1. Every single point of the plane has an inverse, except for the pole O whose inverse is rejected at infinity.
2. If M1 is the inverse of M, then reciprocally M is the inverse of M1.
3. The circle with centre O and radius Vk remains invariant.
4. Any two points and their inverse constitute a quadrangle inscribed on a circle.
5. This circle cuts the invariant circle at a right angle.
6. The quadrilateral of the quadrangle has one external vertex on the centre of the invariant circle.
7. The other external vertex goes on the crossing of the two other opposed sides when M comes into the invariant circle while N keeps remaining outside.

So, what we end up with is the figure of a crossed quadrangle, which I will take as the conceptual equivalent of an ant, in so far as an insect is a crossed, or 'inverted', vertebrate. In my use of this conceptual equivalent, I do not mean to imply that the biological inversion is, strictly speaking, a projective inversion. I am only trying to posit, as Foucault would put it, 'une assise epistemologique commune' – that is, to establish a link between Geoffroy Saint-Hilaire's biology and Gaspard Monge's geometry. I mention the name of Monge rather than that of Poncelet or Brianchon, for three reasons:

Monge rediscovered projective geometry while teaching at the Ecole de Mézières from 1768 to 1783, and began popularising his ideas at the Ecole Normale which, from its inception, was provisionally hosted by the museum where the young Saint-Hilaire had recently arrived. A year or so later, Saint-Hilaire formulated the unity of plan principle.

For Monge, it was essential that the descriptive would become a universal language. As it turns out, he was among those responsible for scientific endeavours during Napoleon's campaign in Egypt. Suffice it to say that he and Saint-Hilaire sailed on the same ship and had plenty of time to talk about their respective interests.

It also happens to be the case that Monge developed projective geometry by teaching stereotomy, and even submitted a proposal for an ellipsoidal vault, the joints of which were lines of curvature, admitting two limit points that he called 'umbilics'. An umbilic is a hybrid concept which, in this case, biology borrowed from geometry. In mathematics, it is a point on a curved surface where all normal sections have the same curvature; in biology, it is the connection between the embryo and the mother through the umbilical cord; which must be knotted after birth.

Inversion and umbilic are only two among many hybrid concepts that exist between biology and geometry. Thus, it makes sense to refer to the terms 'homology' and 'plane of composition' in conjunction with each other. A homology, in projective geometry, is the relationship between two sectional planes of the same visual cone, revolved in order to appear in the same plane. It is then a relationship which appears when one restricts three-dimensional space to a plane. Saint-Hilaire does not use the terms 'homology' and 'analogy' at random. Let us remember the mathematical definition of homology: If, between two figures composed of points and straight lines, one can establish a correspondence so that couples of associated points are located on converging lines, we say that those figures have a centre of homology where the lines converge. However, if the correspondence is such that couples of associated lines intersect at points located on the same line, we would say that this line is the axis of the homology which transforms one figure into another. One founding theorem of projective geometry, formulated by the architect Girard Desargues in 1638, states that, 'if two triangles have a centre of homology, then they have also an axis of homology'.

Such abstract elements as the centre and the axis of homology were exactly the kind of invariant Saint-Hilaire was looking for in continuing the work of his teacher René Just Haüy. He was looking for the plane that would cause an invariant element to materialise, on the basis of which various animals could be said to belong to the same 'forme primitive' in the language of

Haüy or 'Urmotiv' as Semper would say. And from the basis of this unique plane one should be able to generate any species by varying the proportions of an 'Urtier', or original animal structure.

So let us now focus on projective geometry. Perspective was one field of development along with stonecutting and gnomonics. But this new geometry had a much deeper significance in mathematics than just the codification of a practice, since it led to structuring geometry in four storeys: isometry, similitude, projection and topology. The problem is that the history of projective geometry is rather circuitous. It developed independently in the three practical fields mentioned earlier– perspective, stereotomy and gnomonics – until Desargues formulated general theorems to be used in each of the fields.

Although Desargues' work was widely ignored for many years (with the exception of Pascal), it had significantly pervaded several areas of society by the beginning of the 19th century when Semper came to Paris. After Monge's codification of descriptive geometry in 1795, Brianchon would announce in 1810 his astonishing principle of duality, according to which all theorems of geometry have a 'shadow' theorem, which can be deduced by simply replacing the word 'point' with 'straight line', and 'intersect' with 'being aligned'. In 1822 Poncelet published *Traité des propriétés projectives des figures.* Thus it is not surprising that Saint-Hilaire began to think of biology in terms of projective geometry – this was clearly widely discussed among members of the scientific community at that time.

So, to return to our original points of enquiry: what exactly was Semper's understanding of geometry at the *fin de siècle*, and how much did he actually absorb from Gauss? It is difficult to ascertain the answers to these questions. Gauss was known for keeping his work totally secret until he was certain of all of its implications. He rarely revealed the reasoning behind his theorems, and when he published them he made sure that only their final structure was displayed and that all traces up to that point had been hidden. He used to explain that, 'When a beautiful building is finished, one should no longer see the scaffolding.' This sentiment is so close to Semper's own views on architecture that it seems clear evidence of Gauss's influence on his thinking.

It is probable that Semper inherited from Gauss a classical approach to geometry in which Euclid's *Elements* is read as a text oriented towards the platonic theory of polyhedrons, as it is exposed in the *Timée*. Already, his Prolegomenas begin with images of the sphere and the polyhedron as they would appear in crystal. This polygonal concept shows up again in his stereotomy when blocks of stone are conceived as polyedrons. It is clear that Gottfried Semper's views on geometry were an unusual amalgamation. His ideas on textiles clearly anticipate topology and the knot theory, and also revive the main geometrical principle of Anaximander: the apeiron. But his concept of stereotomy is entirely based on the transposition of tectonics into stone and, as such, it remains anchored in a neoclassical reading of Euclid.

Unfortunately, Semper was missing the intermediate space between the polygons of Euclid and the knots of William Thomson. Had he read Desargues, he would have discovered a language of geometry close to the architectural discourse of Philibert de L'Orme. Similar in its knots and stone interlacings; in the projective cone of the trompe d'Anet, and in the vocabulary of its French order: a trunk with knots, branches and thinner ramifications. Instead of restricting his view to regular convex polygons, Semper would have realised that they are a particular case among a whole variety of concave and crossed figures. Moreover, he would have realised that nonregular polygons can actually have interesting projective properties. Take, for example, the alignment of the intersection of the opposed sides as evidenced in Pascal's theorem about the hexagon. Semper would have been even more surprised to find that these projective properties are kept invariant when the polygons happen to be crossed, or degenerated. Geometry takes on a new meaning as long as one does not permit the last chapters of Euclid's *Elements* to bifurcate with Menelaus's theorem. This Greek mathematician of the first century AD, who also initiated spheric trigonometry which provided a Euclidean model of non-Euclidean geometry, established the first projective properties on the basis of Thales' theorem. Moreover, it is possible to calculate all the fundamental theorems of projective geometry – those of Pappus, Ceva, Desargues Pascal and Brianchon – on the basis of this single theorem of Menelaus.

But what lessons can the architects of today learn from Gottfried Semper? Perhaps we are in the same situation as he, piling topology on top of classical geometry while missing the intermediate step. Are we not putting things too simply when we juxtapose the cube with the blob? Is there no other solution than the modernist grid and the contemporary free form? Are we failing to discover supple regularities? Of course, morphing software enables us to link anything with any other thing, but isn't it the process that matters? By simply rejecting the polygons to promote the nurbs, perhaps we are overlooking another geometry for our projects: a projective geometry. ⌂

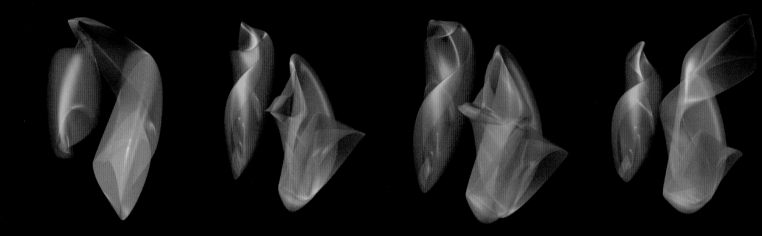

Vigorous Environments

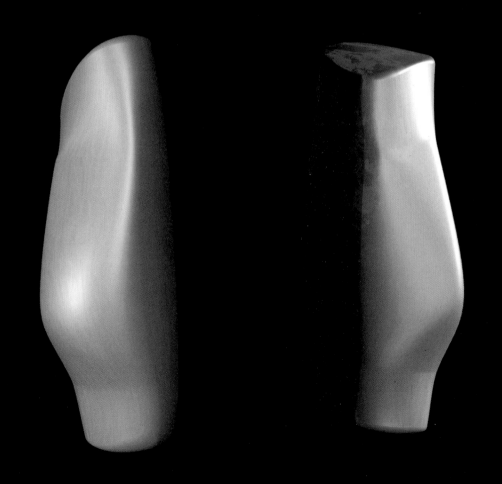

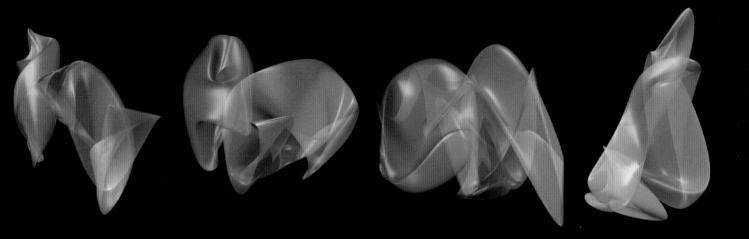

Here **Michael Hensel** and **Kivi Sotama** of the Helsinki-based group OCEAN north describe how they engage in design interventions. Using geometric ambiguity, they shift emphasis away from structure as a static material object towards the temporal and 'dynamic structuration of mobile relations' through space. These formations of open organisation orchestrate different programmatic relationships through different times of inhabitation during the day. The actual interactions that derive from these design interventions are emergent, and act as a link between subject, mileu and intervention.

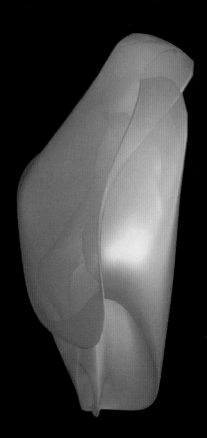

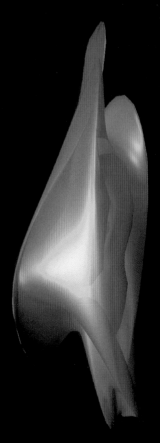

Above top left to right
a_drift *New York Times* time capsules: eight frames of an animation series that draped two linked surfaces around different types of content (not rendered visible here).

Right
a_drift *New York Times* time capsule: digital model of inner ceramic capsule.

Opposite
a_drift *New York Times* time capsules: digital model of outer titanium capsule.

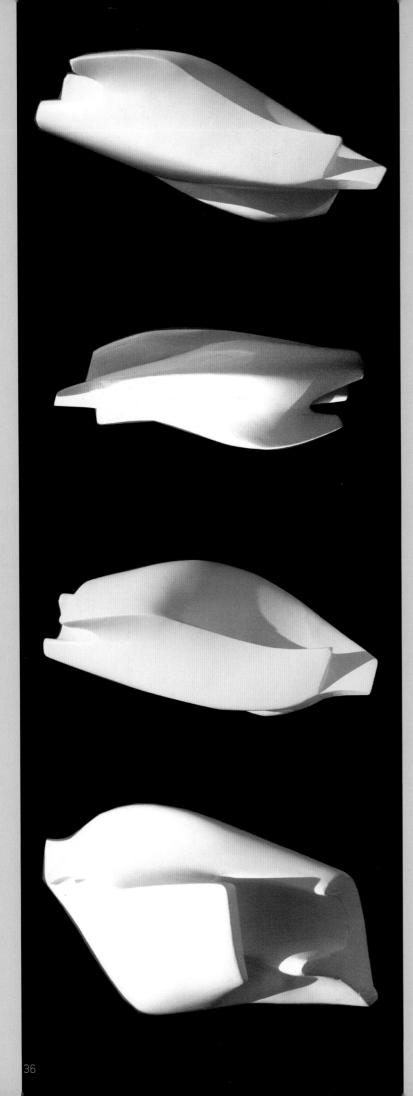

Vigorous Environments
Issues of Performativity and Technology in Design

Vigour n 1 exuberant and resilient strength of body or mind. 2 substantial effective energy or force. 3 forcefulness. 4 the capacity for survival or strong healthy growth in a plant or animal. 5 the most active period or stage of life.

Environment n 1 external conditions or surroundings. 2 Ecology. The external surroundings in which a plant or animal lives, which influences its development and behaviour.

...and if we began to sense that performance embodies such values as efficacy, efficiency, and effectiveness, and to see performers as animal, vegetable, or mineral, distant researchers will experience performance as intensifications in a highly charged atmosphere, as contestations in a cloud of forces ... *Jon McKenzie*

Real change will come not when we turn away from technology toward meaning, but when we recognise the nature of our subordinate position in the technical systems that enroll us, and begin to intervene in the design process in the defense of the conditions of a meaningful life and a liveable environment. *Andrew Feenberg*

Eco-logic

Ecology n 1 the study of the relationships between living organisms and their environment. 2 the set of relationships of a particular organism with its environment.

Today, the increasing complexity of dynamic relations between human activities and hosting milieus renders the fetishisation of discrete and exclusive design objects increasingly futile. This happens to the extent to which the consolidation of the assigned meaning or prescribed functionality of the design-object begins to delimit the interaction between subject and environment. OCEAN north's approach to design emphasises, therefore, the interrelational make-up of the environment as a dynamically unfolding generative field, and suggests an organisational paradigm for design rooted in a radical shift towards a primacy of process over events, of relationships over entities and of development over structure. In doing so this approach seeks to engender relational dynamics between material form, ambient conditions, social arrangements, habitational potential and the subject – individual as well as collective. Consequentially, this approach necessitates the inclusion of indeterminable, unforeseeable influences and inevitable contingencies and accidents that invigorate dynamic milieus. Consequently, any notion of contingency implies issues of noncontrollability and freely evolving conditions, and is in opposition to traditional approaches to design which require the assertion of hard control over (relationships between)

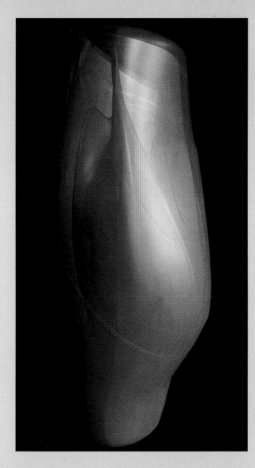

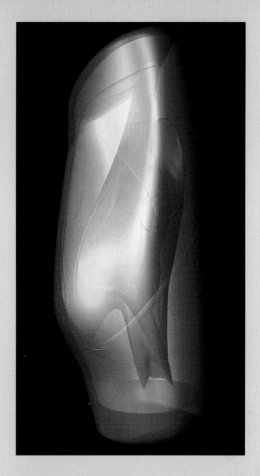

matter and functionality. Regulating relational dynamics entails temporal interventions in processes and the establishment of loose affiliations between conditions, as well as their (combined) feedback effect upon the intervention. Feedback informs, then, the careful modification of the regulatory influence and changes the kind and degree of control over the transformation of the milieu.

From this position three questions arise in pursuit of the ecological design paradigm:

1. To which degree can design control be suspended or relinquished? Within the ecological design paradigm the role of control must shift, from consolidating stable alignments and characteristics between constituent elements within a milieu towards temporal regulation of generative processes which are in exchange with both local and combined dynamics of the environment. Hence, even though a degree of control is asserted over local spatiotemporal regions, this is done in contact with, and under the impact of, reregulating contingent forces from within the milieu. Interventions become less motivated as permanent impositions of will and control and are, rather, provisional mediating and mediated processes of exchange.

2. How can relational dynamics be regulated without reinstigating inflexible forms of hard control? Because of dynamic feedback relations, each point in time becomes a potential generative juncture through which a mobile structure of time is established that suggests that provisional spatiotemporal design operations must become the predominant

instrumental mode of intervention. The traditional axis of hypothesis–analysis–synthesis becomes eroded by the fact that perpetual transformation takes place across the entire generative milieu – ever restless and becoming. Ongoing analysis must therefore inform provisional intervention in exchanges with the environment, in turn renecessitating analysis, time and again.

3. How can the dynamics of evolving environments be facilitated to produce – in an instrumental way – responsive conditions and synergetic effects? This question requires the careful repositioning of the role of technology as a facilitator of transformative processes. While the role of technology as a facilitator of 'interactivity' might have become a contemporary cliché, the important issue is the realisation that interactivity as a two-way transfer of information establishes the necessary precondition for synergy and feedback as core functions of performativity.

Performativity

To study performance is not to focus on complete forms, but to become aware of performance as itself a contested space ... *Elin Diamond*

In order to arrive at a notion of interactivity, beyond the cliché, it is important to investigate possible concepts, methods and mechanisms for establishing dynamic feedback relations between the subject and a milieu before turning to a discussion on the role of technology within the ecological design paradigm. The question that must be asked, then, is what types of phenomena and mechanisms of exchange underlie and catalyse dynamic feedback relations between the subject and the milieu; and how can an instrumental approach be formulated from this position.

Opposite
a_drift *New York Times* time capsules: plaster model of inner ceramic capsule.

Above
a_drift *New York Times* time capsules: 'x-ray' rendering; digital model showing inner ceramic capsule nested in outer titanium capsule.

An important reference to answering this question in relation to OCEAN north's research is Umberto Eco's seminal work *Opera Aperta* (The open work) in which he posits a notion of the openness of a work (of art) yielded by its deliberate ambiguity. This implies in other words a plurality and multiplicity of orders, which in turn give rise to, and catalyse interactions between, a work and the perceiving subject. Eco suggests that such works in motion leave the arrangement of some of their constituents to the public or to chance, thus giving these works a field of possible orders rather than a single definite one. The beholder (subject) can move freely within this field, which is engendered by a degree of ambiguity in the work, as a means of avoiding conventional forms of expression and therefore prescribed interpretation. However, Eco continues to argue, the interpretation of an open work must be far from entirely free and a formative intention, which must seek to direct

into a nondecomposable surface in order to arrive at a composite geometry free of referential associations to any existing furniture types. Computational modelling enabled the rapid reassemblage of the sampled geometries in order to assess the latent ergonomic capacity of the resultant composite geometry. The final piece was made of vacuum-formed sheets of ABS-plastic reinforced with a 5-millimetre layer of high-density polyurethane, and its specifically emerging pattern of use and cohabitation was tested on various social occasions. These tests showed that Extraterrain's utilisation and usefulness depended entirely on the engagement of the user with the surface, in negotiation with whoever else occupied the piece at the same time. The heterogeneous geometry of the piece destabilised simple divisions between spaces that could be individually occupied, and necessitated ongoing territorial negotiation between simultaneous users. In this way geometry and positioning trigger incidental individual use and the array of individual use accumulates to collective interaction. The latter

Eco suggests that such works in motion leave the arrangement of some of their constituents to the public or to chance, thus giving these works a field of possible orders rather than a single definite one.

the responses of the subject, must be manifest in each work.

In pursuing Eco's notion of works in motion OCEAN north attempts to uncouple geometric articulation of the material systems of the milieu from the deliberate encoding of implied meaning. In order to instil an operative ambiguity of meaning, it pursues computational methods of sampling and fusing partial geometries into unfamiliar and nondecomposable geometric composites. This operation enables the removal of typological references from the resultant form and the space defined by it. In replacing meaning as the predominant operative encoding of geometry, emergent orders can thereafter arise from the real-time interaction between the space defined by the new composite form, and its occupants. Geometric ambiguity shifts the emphasis from structure as static material arrangement to the dynamic structuration of mobile relations in time and across space. One example of this approach is the Extraterrain furniture project (1996), which aimed at charging a simple material surface with varied potential for occupation and use, while simultaneously evading any prescription or indication of a proper use. Diverse sectional geometries were digitally sampled and fused

constitutes an unfolding of a field of social interactions facilitated by the geometric articulation of Extraterrain.

Hence, interventions along the ecological design paradigm proceed through setting out fields of possible arrangements. These generative fields emanate from the varied tensions between nonprescriptive, yet directed, relations between design interventions, the milieu and the subject in a continual process of de- and restabilisation of the relationships between them. The actual elements of emergent affiliations between intervention, milieu and subject are the milieu's manifold formal, material and ambient effects perceived by the subject and, in return, the actual affects and reactions of the subject to these effects and their combined impact upon the milieu. Performativity arises from perpetual feedback relations between the subject and the milieu. It is crucial, however, to distinguish between the concept of the *Gesamtkunstwerk* as a totality and notions of designing with relational dynamics. The difference is simply the ability of the latter to incorporate contingency and the accidental in the generative process. In doing so, performativity gives primacy to formation over gestalt, to dynamic multiplicity over finite totality.

Technology
How, then, are these notions of cultural and social performance related to notions of technological

Opposite
a_drift *New York Times* time capsules: rapid prototype model showing inner ceramic capsule nested in outer titanium capsule.

39

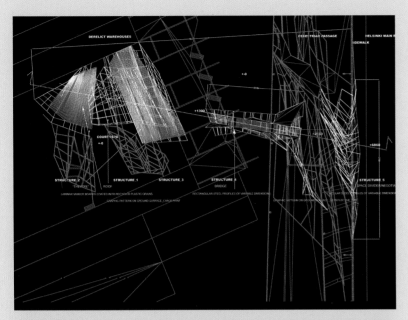

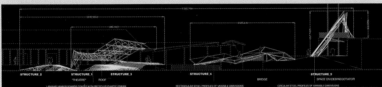

performance, which serves to guide and optimise the design, testing and manufacturing of industrial and consumer commodities of all kinds? There is a contradiction between product optimisation and formative processes open to contingency only if product and formative process are understood as separated conditions, and if optimisation refers to a set of static requirements to be answered with a singular and finite product for all times. When an open formative process of production becomes the product, when optimisation becomes a way of evolving possibilities for individualised spatiotemporal experience, the contradiction begins to erode. Obviously, some of this has long been recognised by the commercial apparatus that today strategically changes brands, products and services at an ever-faster rate. The apparent individualisation of goods and commodities proceeds, however, still through the limited assemblage of catalogued and finite products along the lines of Post-modern collage. The question remains as to how to arrive at a dynamically evolving production of nonprescribed possibilities. Here the role of technology must be rethought as both substrate and catalyst for new types of dynamic and divergent production processes, with

performativity being its condition and aim. Current technology can provide the ubiquitous enabling infrastructure that can facilitate real-time exchange between subject and milieu, and yield a generative immersive field of material and ambient effects that affects, and is in turn affected by, interaction. If modes of production become the product within the new design paradigm, then design and its implementation can no longer be separated. The same technologies that facilitate the conceptualisation and undertaking of interventions along the new paradigm must also then become the eventual infrastructure of the production of effects and the exchange between subject and diverse aspects and systems of the milieu.

Intervening in Vigorous Environments

In 1999 the *New York Times* organised a competition for the design of a time capsule required to last 1,000 years, located on American territory. The content of the capsule was to be specified by the newspapers' readers as a selection of items that would communicate our culture at the close of the second millennium.

OCEAN north's finalist entry strategised an approach that facilitated the design of an unlimited number of variations on one generic design solution. Each one of nine capsules consisted of an inner and an outer capsule, and was configured around two inner chambers nested within the inner capsule. The form of the chambers emerged from the specific set of items contained within. This was achieved by the use of a digital animation method that draped surfaces around each specific set of items, evolving in this way the form of the inner capsule. With each new set of contents a new form emerged that made each inner capsule a highly individual derivation of the same family. The outer titanium shell was then draped around the inner capsule and its form adjusted for aquadynamic performance. Moving outwards from the form of the content at the core of the capsule, the resonance in the geometry became weaker and was gradually transformed into a barely recognisable deformation of the outer titanium shell. In this manner, the nine capsules were but examples of an indefinite virtual series of potential capsules.

The inner capsule was to be made of a carbon-fibre-reinforced ceramic composite, employing processing technologies that enable the fabrication of complex geometry without damage to the fibre. The titanium for the outer capsule was to be manufactured in two deep-drawn pieces and welded together. In this way the capsules would be carriers of information, able to convey the design sensibility and technological and material manufacturing capability of our culture.

After their production, the capsules were to be filled and sealed in New York before being transported to the Antarctic and buried in nine different ice-bound

locations. The initial location, the ice of the polar caps, is the slowest-changing domain of the oceanic milieu. As the oceans, and their coldest regions, endure change they offer an appropriate location for the preservation of the time-capsule project.

The capsules would be contained in the ice until natural glacial movements and melting dispatched the units into the sea water. A monitoring system, which would register the movement of the capsules in the oceans once they were released from the ice, was to be installed in New York. Signals would be transmitted from the capsules by a system empowered by sea-water batteries.

The future of the capsules would be dependent on their possible release from their entombment in the ice, their respective journeys within the oceanic currents and their possible discovery by future cultures. Because the capsules would be subjected to forces of transience and change, their destiny would be unpredictable. Rather than prescribing control and monumentality, the project engaged the processes of time that motivated its conception. The scale of the receptacles was directly opposite to that of a monument – but the trajectory of each would have been monumental in its planetary vastness in space, time and engagement of chance.

The plurality of the approach allowed for the possible arrival of the capsules at some destination in the far future, without privileging one destination over another, and enabled their transmitting variegated and nuanced information about our culture.

Designing Vigorous Environments

The *Intencities Installation* (2000) was designed as part of the Helsinki Cultural Capital 2000 events. The site for the intervention was Makasiini, a 19th-century U-shaped and single-storey block of ex-railway depots facing the Finnish House of Parliament and Kiasma – Stephen Holl's Museum of Modern Art. The aim of the intervention was to further pursue research into designing with relational dynamics by means of deploying a broad scope of conditions, elements and relational tactics in order to achieve a rich pallet of interactions. The intervention incorporated elements of art, architecture, dance, music, media and graphic design. The multidisciplinary design team devised a loosely coupled choreographic layout to engender dynamic interactions between scheduled performances, and defined formal,

sonic, tactile and material elements and emergent flows of movement and ambient effects across the site. The architectural component of the intervention featured five geometrically differentiated structures made of steel tube, timber planks and plastic film.

While the structures made loose provision for programmatic arrangements, such as stages, seating or circulation areas, viewing platforms and bridges, none of these was evident from their formal articulation. These structures revealed their occupational potential only through the staging of events and artistic performances, much like the Extraterrain project. The utilisation of the structures emerged from their spontaneous use by the performers, visitors and audiences. The construction and surfacing of the structures undertaken over time, changing their appearance and presence in the site. Motion-triggered light and sound systems were integrated into the structures and enabled feedback between visitors and the changing ambient effects of the intervention. In acting as a projection surface, the structures configured an audiovisually animated landscape as well as both stage and backdrop for the different events and performances. The introduction of new media technology served to translate physical movement across the site into digital animations, which were projected on to the surfaces of the structures. The visitors could use both their actual movement and their mobile phones to manipulate the projected graphics, and therefore the audiovisual appearance of the intervention.

The dance performances evolved randomly in relation to visitor movement and participation. The initial distance and distinction between dancer and audience decreased gradually as the dancers moved into, through and with the audience. In this way, the initial relationship was reversed and yielded participation of visitors in the performances. In addition, real-time surface painting was linked with the dance performance and the visitors' movements. Tracing the various movements of dancers and visitors, the painter created layer upon layer of markings. In doing so, the painter became, variously, an integral part of the dance performance and, at other times, a random follower of the visitors' movements, light intensities, density of media projections or sound impulses. The differentiated geometry of the material construct and the changing intensities of ambient effects, as well as the individual and collective movement of visitors and performers, continually converged and diverged, provisionally assembling and dispersing the elements of the intervention into ever-changing configurations. The built and ambient environment, events and deployed technology, jointly produced a field of conditions and effects animated by collective inhabitation – vigorous and performative. ∆

Opposite top to bottom
Intencities Installation: plan view of structures 1–5.

Intencities Installation: sectional elevation of structures 1–5.

Intencities Installation: view of structure 5 during a dance performance.

Above
Intencities Installation: views of structure 5.

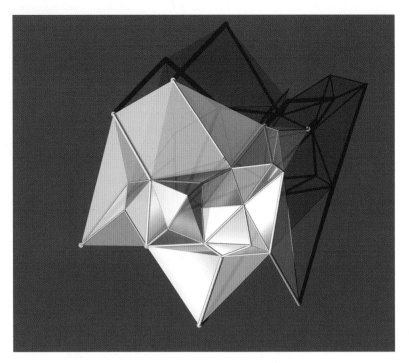

Creating Synthesis Partners

Contemporary techniques are process-based, and relate to material objects as dynamic organisations that challenge the stasis of the formal object. **Kristina Shea** has created a prototype system of synthesis techniques called eifForm that relates material objects to aspects of geometry, topology and principles of structural engineering. This has the effect of moving the work away from material specialisations and restrictions, or specific applications, and allows for interaction with dynamic processes that contribute to the rapid generation of design alternatives. These new computational techniques lead to the creation of innovative discrete structures and the incorporation of performance indicators beyond structural mass. According to Shea, one measure of the effectiveness of contemporary techniques lies in their ability to rapidly analyse the performance of newly modified design forms and functions.

Computational techniques continue to impact the world of design: what we can design, what we can fabricate and construct and, as a result, even what we imagine. To date, software for architectural and engineering design has progressed from coarse drafting systems to powerful tools that incorporate solid modelling and a wide range of analytical capabilities. Current tools help us to easily create and modify accurate digital models of our ideas, as well as to evaluate aspects of their manufacturing feasibility. However, these tools are limited to modelling our own ideas, rather than actively contributing to rapid generation of design alternatives – beyond our own insight. Fortunately, computational techniques aimed at creating synthesis partners are now emerging.

The relation between geometry and structure is dynamic, changing as new materials arrive and fabrication and construction techniques advance. If a structure 'looks right' is it always right? How about in the reverse case?

Computational analysis is essential to the design of modern structures with modern materials. As a tool for retrospective study, it can be used to understand past design, and to challenge the rationale and rules it used. To give an example, the wooden bridges proposed by Palladio in his third book seem to have been created as two joining cantilevers based on an increase in the section proposed – from the support to the centre along the bottom chord. However, further analysis has shown that the bridge could not have acted that way and that, in fact, the forces increase along the bottom chord rather than decrease. Palladio used rules for relating structure and form based on intuition about force flow, stability and structural economy. Heuristics, rules of thumb and analogy will always play a key role in structural studies. For example, Calatrava speaks of making toys to study intriguing relations between structure and form. But through the use of computation we can now challenge our assumptions about traditional relations in order to uncover factors that drive standard designs and new relations for the future. The technique discussed in this article, implemented in a prototype system called eifForm, provides a starting point for exploring the potential of synthesis partners for generating conventional and novel free-form discrete structures.

Minimal Discrete Forms

People have been interested in minimal structural forms since as early as 1864 when Maxwell determined the analytic solution of a minimum mass cantilever. The solution was an infinite field of orthogonal tension and compression members. Since this design was difficult to realise the method was adjusted by Prager in 1977 to consider joint weight. A series of designs that trade off structural mass and number of joints resulted, where the spectrum spans from the infinite analytic solution to a three-member design. While analytic techniques provide understanding of the nature of optimal discrete structural forms, further practical limitations, such as buckling, make practical application difficult.

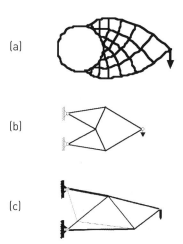

(a)

(b)

(c)

The aerospace and automotive industries have begun to integrate structural topology optimisation and analysis early in the design process. Is there a place for it in architectural and structural design? A key challenge stems from the emphasis on design as art, which is less dominant in other industries . Here subjective performance goals of composition and aesthetics often prevail.

eifForm

Creating effective computational synthesis techniques requires the development of new ways to represent and intelligently modify both the form and function of designs, as well as to rapidly analyse their performance. Designers often describe the use of nonlinear and nonmonotonic processes as a key element for

achieving creative and innovative solutions. The same is generally true for computational design processes. Techniques using monotonic processes, such as expert systems and traditional optimisation, are generally targeted at routine design tasks. But, as shown by the recent development of design techniques using stochastic and evolutionary methods, a nonmonotonic process, combined with a rich geometric representation, offers possibilities for generating novel designs with intriguing geometry.

eifForm contributes to the trend of integrated design, taking advantage of analytical techniques and computing speed to create a performance-based system of structural synthesis. The technique, called structural shape annealing, combines grammatical shape generation, performance evaluation and simulated annealing, a stochastic optimisation technique. Initially compared to benchmark results in structural topology optimisation, the method was shown to be capable of generating innovative, optimally directed planar trusses and single-layer space frames. It has also been successfully used in an investigation of transmission tower redesign for an energy company.

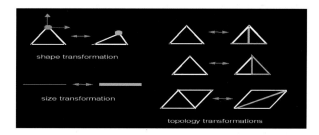

While this study illustrated the potential for using the technique for highly constrained structural design problems, the focus in this article is to explore underconstrained design spaces, and the potential for generating rational architectural forms.

In this context, the aim of the technique is to generate functionally sound design possibilities that are beyond the designer's concepts of what is possible. Taking the viewpoint that form is function, a structural grammar is used to represent the relationship between form and function found in truss structures through the specification of allowable structural transformations. One way of employing the rules is to hand-select and apply them to an initial design to generate known designs for the modelled structural class – for example, the generation of a Warren truss. But, when transformations are applied iteratively in random order at random locations in the design, the set of transformations defines an infinite language of structural shapes. A key aspect of the structural grammar is to ensure that each design in the language can be mapped to a valid analytic model in order to assess structural performance. Currently, structural forms are always interpreted as truss structures with

Above left
Minimal discrete forms: (a) form proposed by Michell (1904); (b) practical variation proposed by Prager (1977); (c) same topology generated by eifForm (2001).

Above right
Structural grammar for planar trusses.

Opposite
Free-form pavilion generated to cover a space defined by eight different height support locations.

43

idealised pin-joints, using prescribed material properties and section shapes.

Moving a structural topology optimisation method towards practicality in architecture requires incorporating a wide range of performance indicators beyond structural mass alone. Each structure generated is interpreted using computable metrics for efficiency, economy, usage and aesthetics to evaluate both geometry and behaviour. Structural performance is assessed with respect to acceptable limits on stress, buckling and displacement. The overall performance of a design is then calculated as a weighted summation of defined metrics where the weights reflect trade-offs among objectives. This provides a means to choose among designs in the described language.

The process of structural generation in eifForm is not modelled after a conventional design process or linked to a specific material. Rather than using a predefined sequence for generating the structural form, the method applies near-randomly selected rules in near-randomly selected locations. The stochastic nature of the process enables innovative designs to evolve through a series of design transformations as a response to the modelled design scenario and loading model. To direct the search, rather than just randomly picking designs in the defined language, the method uses control techniques for selecting which rule to use when and where.

Rethinking the Planar Truss

Structure is often considered after the conceptualisation of form and can be seen to hinder creativity and innovation. To illustrate how a synthesis tool could improve the dialogue between form creation and structural realisation, let us return to fundamentals and rethink the planar roof truss. As part of a structural study we would like to explore different systems of planar trusses. Given a span from the form under study, conventional triangulation schemes – Warren, Pratt, Fink, etc – are considered along with options of parallel, angled or bowed chords. We choose the one that seems appropriate, or looks right, and assume that the chosen system can eventually be made to work through member-sizing.

What if we reverse the process and drive the form concept from the structural study? Using eifForm, a range of lightweight, simply supported trusses can be generated for three different spans – 30, 45 and 60 metres – using variable size steel tubes. The truss variants created are

responses to a uniform load, the weight of the covering material distributed to a limited number of equally spaced connection points across the top chord. Stress and buckling limitations are adhered to. Allowing generation of an infinitely deep truss, the structure stretches down to reduce the stresses in members. Symmetry is maintained in some of the design generations but, when unconstrained, asymmetric forms emerge. While the lightest designs generated for each span were symmetric, symmetry can give the illusion of lightness while being heavier than some clumsier looking asymmetric variants. By maintaining a line of symmetry in the asymmetric designs these can be split along the centre line to study the two halves. We would expect symmetric forms to emerge for a symmetric loading but deep asymmetric designs emerge where the two halves are nearly equivalent in mass. This illustrates the existence of, and capacity for generating, multiple equally efficient designs for underconstrained scenarios.

eifForm generates discrete structures in response to a prescribed generation and search model. If we place a uniform constraint on the depth of the truss across all three spans, ranging from 1/7 to 1/14 for individual spans, the process produces more practical variants. As a stochastic technique is used, a range of similar quality designs can be generated from the same search model. While the designs are somewhat unconventional, the variation in member size can be used to interpret the flow of forces relative to the loading model. Common patterns are often found among generated designs as a result of the structural language defined by the shape grammar. This language of designs can be modified and expanded through the addition of new rules, modelling new styles.

Onwards and Upwards ... 2.5D

The synthesis technique is based on fundamental aspects of geometry, topology and structural principles rather than being specialised for certain materials or application domains. It is easily extended to generate 2.5D structures, ie single-layer space trusses. Constraining the planar topology to a purely triangulated space with no overlapping members, 3D enclosures can be generated by prescribing a projection surface such as a hemisphere. Extending the previous planar rules through a study of patterns found in geodesic domes, pseudogeodesic domes were generated that have a 30 metre diameter base. Symmetric and asymmetric responses to multiple independent symmetric and asymmetric loads are possible. Designs illustrate the impact of changing the performance model, which drives search direction. A lightweight option with little enclosure space is generated, while a pseudogeodesic design emerges from the addition of performance metrics for minimising surface area, maximising enclosure space

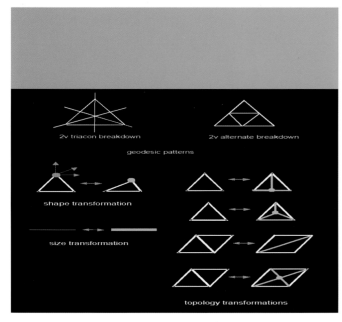

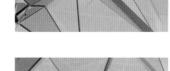

and uniformity of the surface subdivision.

While based on geodesic patterns, the same structural grammar can be used in combination with other surfaces and spaces. A conoidal roof is used to cover an octagonal aeroplane hangar, roughly 50 × 50 metres, a more cost-effective proposal over rectangular hangars. A conoid is prescribed over the octagonal perimeter to provide high clearance only at one end of the hangar to accommodate the aeroplane tail. The structure shown uses steel tubes and is a minimum mass response to self-weight and distributed surface loads associated with snow and roofing material. The golden ratio, a geometric proportion often related to structural efficiency, is used as an aesthetic performance measure to direct generation towards golden triangle patterns. While each is unique on its own, the asymmetric pods can be arranged into clusters of hangars to create a balance between uniformity and diversity.

Rational Free Forms?

Removing the definition of the projection surface, eifForm can also be used for conceptualisation of triangulated free forms by allowing each point to be projected independently. Rather than creating the form and then considering structural options, structure is now treated explicitly and drives the definition of the exterior and interior form. The figure of the free-form pavilion on page 42 considers the challenge of creating a structure to span a roughly 28 × 29 metre space defined by eight support points of different heights stemming from limited connection locations in a difficult site, or simply to create a desired program or style. The designs produced are visually different but have similar structural efficiency in response to self-weight and surface loading. A peak arises from requiring the structure to achieve a certain height, at least at one point. Endless variations of scenario models can be explored; and for underconstrained

problems many functionally sound possibilities can be rapidly generated. using an inside-out design process, generated forms are used to stimulate new programs that can be incorporated in the process to constrain or direct the generation towards designs that reflect specific intent.

Expanding Digital Design Processes

It is difficult to separate new techniques and processes since, through their development, we aim to enhance current practice. Synthesis tools add a new component to current digital processes but should be tightly integrated with CAD tools, digital topography maps and material databases for creating initial scenarios. As computation speed increases, the level of interaction possible with performance-based synthesis techniques, such as eifForm, increases to strengthen the partnership between designer and technique. As the resulting designs often lie beyond the experience of the designer, proper interpretation is essential for better understanding and use of the technique. Using generated designs for more than stimuli, it is important that interpretation is made, with respect to the underlying structural model, through use of analysis and contextual visualisation tools. The designs shown are rational – structurally speaking – only with respect to the structural model used for generation. As with any design process iteration is essential, and through refinement of models and further generation a better understanding of the relation between performance models and form can be achieved. To investigate buildability issues, designs can be transferred to rapid prototyping tools.

What's Next?

The convergence of expressive CAD tools, improved analysis methods and advanced fabrication and construction techniques has enabled both increased freedom of expression in form and structure, and more realistic assessment of innovative design alternatives. It is hoped that emerging synthesis tools such as eifForm will widen the range and number of rational forms considered and, through enhanced performance models, lead to both innovative and buildable designs. Extending the implemented structural grammars to include further structural typologies and approximate evaluation techniques will create a computational partner for dynamic study of what-if scenarios. The true power of synthesis partners will be seen only when designers can easily customise the system, defining their own generative style through structural transformations, geometric constraints and performance metrics. It is important to note that synthesis tools aim to become partners, not designers or engineers, to blend with human creativity – not replace it – so that we can expand our insight and realise our imaginations. ⌂

The Digital and
the Material

Cecil Balmond in conversation with Michael Weinstock

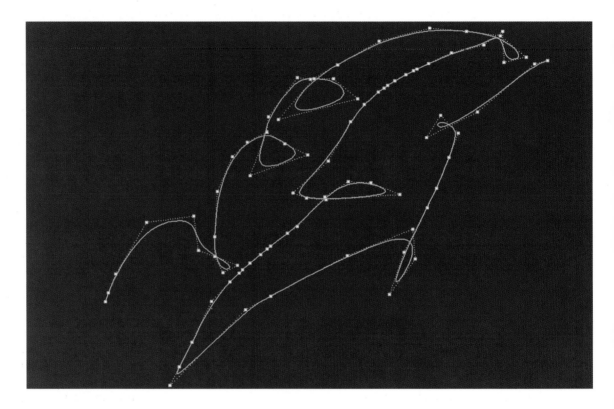

As chairman of the operations board at Ove Arup, heading the advanced geometry group, structural engineer **Cecil Balmond** holds an iconic position in contemporary architecture. Having worked constantly at the forefront of the field, he has collaborated with the most innovative and experimental of three generations of architects: Philip Johnson, Toyo Ito, Rem Koolhaas, Daniel Libeskind and Ben Van Berkel. **Michael Weinstock**, who has a special interest in emergent technologies and is Master of Technical Studies at the Architecture Association in London, interviewed Balmond. Focusing on Balmond's pioneering role at the intersection of the digital and the material, they discuss how this has manifested itself in his collaborative work and his application of construction techniques, as well as how it relates to his wider philosophy and scientific preoccupations.

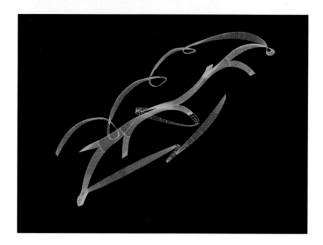

Digital technologies have had a profound effect on the world, implementing a radical change to the concepts and working practices of art, science and industry. Yet in architecture they remain, as yet, largely immaterial. Perhaps the most visible manifestation of the new technologies is the explosion of digital experiments that have in common 'free forms'. The 'digiterati' often seem to be legitimising their practice by claiming to be inhabiting a future production paradigm. I asked Cecil Balmond, who moves freely between the digital and the material, about these claims.

'I have a wider view and do not feel that I am to be completely associated with the digital. Not all of my work is digital, but I do use it a lot and see it as part of a whole process. My process is pretty constant; I start with sketching the space, however impossible that space is to draw. It is essential for me to try to capture the thought at the very beginning. Then I use the computer. The digital opens horizons, and refines intuition. I cannot explain why I choose a particular algorithm to explore. Intuition, which works best in an otherwise rigorous process, is knowing where to look.

There are many proposals of free forms, or 'blobs', which appear very seductive on the computer screen. Interesting as they are, there is not much point when the result is surfaces that are essentially cladding. Structure is then needed to underpin the shape, and a lot of structural work has to be done in order to make the spaces viable. This experimental work was important, and deserves respect, but it will remain a fad unless it takes on a structural integrity. I prefer that fold and curvature can have a meaning that will draw structural materiality to those forms.

No method is wholly good or bad, but it is essential that there is a self-consistent framework to the solution. We have to develop an appropriate approach that interrelates structure with material and programme. There needs to be more rigour in the process itself. A consistent vision is needed, with an associated theory, and a deeper collaboration with the construction industry and manufacturing processes. I hope that the work we do here in my group of advanced geometry at Arup will help to push this agenda.'

The list of architects that Cecil has worked with includes the most successful, famous and experimental of three generations: Johnson, Koolhaas, Ito, Libeskind and Van Berkel amongst many others. His preference for working in

collaboration requires a trust and an engagement with each other's sensibilities of design. It demands a commitment to going beyond thinking of structure and architecture as separate categories, and finding a way of working that includes both but is more.

'The area that we jointly focus on is the space of imagination, and that extends beyond technicalities. My interest in collaboration started a long time ago, from the period of my early work with Rem Koolhaas. Rem seemed to be someone with an open agenda, highly speculative and aggressive about the contemporary condition. We got on very well, because I was also struggling at that time to break out of the straitjacket that engineering thinking had got me into. Those early works were highly definitive for me, opening up possibilities, and our method was truly collaborative. We worked like design partners and some key work came out of that collaboration. Many of the projects are unbuilt, sadly, particularly Zebrugge and Jussieu which I liked so much at the time.

I was looking for more open territory then, because many architects had traditional notions of architecture, a particular concern for a grand plan, for an aesthetic of objecthood. With Koolhaas and Libeskind and van Berkel I work like this, closely, sometimes you can't put a piece of paper between us. Part of being a collaborator is being an aspiring partner. I can work with different demands but my quest for exploring new configuration is systematic and constant. And I am always learning. The years of collaboration mean that the exchange is subtle and complex. With Ben Van Berkel for instance there is a common understanding of the dynamic of plan and section in one seamlessness'

Shipbuilders have almost completely eliminated drawings, and work as closely as they can to a comprehensive three-dimensional digital model. This suggests that building-production dialogues must change, and that there will be radical revisions to the way architects work. The old method of completely preparing a project before sending it out to tender will have to give way to a more collaborative process, and very early relations with all parties including the contractor. Cecil thinks that there will be great changes, and some are already here.

'In the construction of the V&A, for example, there won't be conventional drawings. There will be no paper, but fully documented three-dimensional models on CD. There will be global axes for setting out the site, but only local references as the construction moves up the spiral.

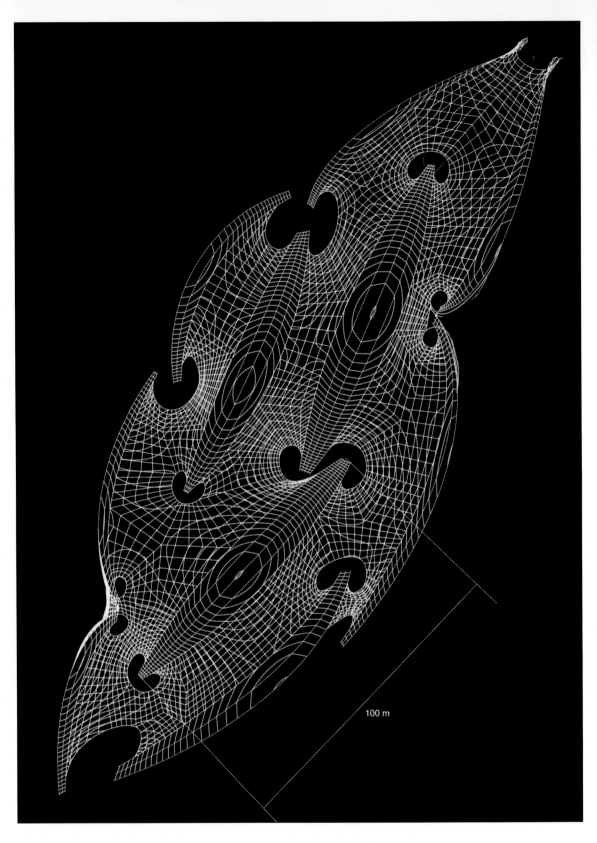

100 m

In the future we will have a digital model, then go directly to CADCAM manufacturing processes. The old system of production comprised a series of quite separate actions. I doubt that this works with complex surface-modelled projects. This kind of project particularly requires that you work as a team, and procurement has to have different strategies. Collaboration is the key.'

There is now an almost unrestricted access to information, and this contributes to the breakdown of barriers between disciplines, a dismantling of the 'professional' protection of separate and specialised practices and the emergence of integrated, multidisciplined 'designer' practices. Cecil takes the view that there can't be a 'Renaissance' designer who can cover all areas of work, as it would be impossible for a single person to do so much. He stresses the need for highly integrated teams with many different skills, driven by an engine of information process.

'Landscape, urbanscape, building scapes can all be thought of as 'infoscape'. In the early days of the new techniques I gave a lecture at Yale, and a landscape architect asked me if I realised that these techniques could be applied to lage landscape. Similarly, urbanists began to talk to me about the growth patterns in cities. Once those connections are made, it becomes evident to me that what is possible is a much broader coalition, of generic processes that involve the same layer of information, working at different scales, connected by inner hierarchies of logic. Ultimately it is about the serial orders of pattern.'

This is what a structural biologist might describe as the primary programming of self-ordering and self-assembly. There have been quite radical revisions to conceptual schema of 'nature', from the concept of a mechanism to a more systemic concept of organism. As biologists have become engaged in complexity theory and in emergent behaviours, it was inevitable that architecture would become engaged with these ideas. I asked Cecil if this had influenced his way of working.

'Absolutely. What fascinated me was the tenet of complexity theory, feedback not copyback! I do have a scientific background and I returned to chemistry and biology, and studied them in more depth than I had in the past. I found evidence of complex processes in nature, and wanted to understand how they work. I studied silicates, blood haemoglobin and the spirals of DNA. A conviction grew in me that a method of design

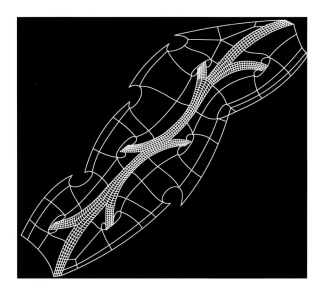

There is an important section in Cecil Balmond's book *Number 9*[1] in which he uses four conceptual mirrors to perform operations. They work in a way that reminds me of Duchamp, who was the first person to use the word 'virtual'. He used the term to refer to a dimension in which appearance could not be apprehended by a viewer, except by the mediation of arcane geometries. There is a shared interest in how things reflect and invert as they are taken across conceptual boundaries, in serial repetition, and a sense of play in mathematics. I asked Cecil what effect writing the book had on his work.

There have been quite radical revisions to conceptual schema of 'nature', from the concept of a mechanism to a more systemic concept of organism. As biologists have become engaged in complexity theory and in emergent behaviours, it was inevitable that architecture would become engaged with these ideas.

could be evolved that had within it the capacity for chance. It took a long time for me to trust this idea. It wasn't easy to abandon the deductive logic of my training and work on inductive processes. But I found them to be very satisfying, and my interest in nonlinear processes also connects to my work in numbers. Numbers have preoccupied me for many years, and I find there are architectural and spatial events, too, in numbers. In particular I have found studying primes to be very fruitful. My entire faith in serial work rises from the prime numbers, which are the most abstract and perfect manifestation of aperiodicity.'

'The book embraces the rational but surprisingly produces a mystery of the irrational. I like to seed such thoughts into my work if possible. I love magic, which may be because of my Sri Lankan background. Magic means to me the sense of finding surprise and delight in the process of working. A sense of play is important if work is to go forward. The development of my work proceeded from geometry, which led me to pattern. The irony was that as an engineer I was supposed to know about geometry. Yet I found that I knew nothing and needed to refresh the sources of my knowledge. What intrigued me were the animate aspects of geometry and that's where my research and efforts have been concentrated over the last 15 years.

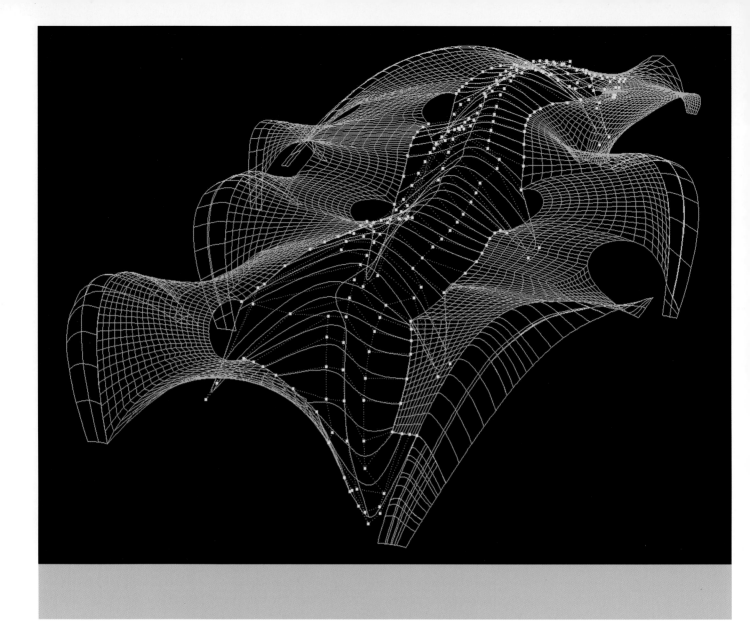

Above
Detailed form with
controlled surface.

Opposite
Final material form.

It was widely expected of me that I would write first about my work in architecture. What came first, however, was setting up a new agenda, and the book ends with the very process that I now use in my work. *Number 9* started with an interest in the graphic consequences of quite arid mathematical formulae for solutions to number puzzles. This gave me the first mandala,[2] which is concentric, logical and symmetrical. This was enough for me to start the book, but in the writing there was a sudden realisation that the data contained something else that contradicted this symmetry. The second mandala is dynamic, just caught at one moment in its spin.'

In the book the lesson of the second mandala is that 'we need not fear the apparent disjointed and twisted surfaces of the non-symmetric'. This is clearly a manifesto, powerfully resonant with Balmond's work in experimental architecture and structures.

'Structure starts with a single punctuation, as for example a simple column in space. It has the particular asymmetry of an individual act, so the next act becomes a rhythmic juxtaposition. I like to think of structure as episodic or as travelling margin. In the generic sense, architecture concerns movement, memory and the actuation of the social, but it is structure that acts as a catalyst to form and space. Nonlinear techniques lead to transformations, and I find this unpredictable dynamic produces interesting new manifestations of architecture.

Cecil Balmond's work has at its root the empowerment of an animated geometry, refined over a long period and in which distinctions between structure and space are redundant. There is a contagious excitement in his deep engagement with building new forms and spaces, and in his fundamental belief in the opportunities of the next project. I expect his current work in progress with the materialist Shigeru Ban to reveal a new azimuth on this trajectory.

Form, materials, space and structure are traditionally discussed as discrete subjects. Cecil's strong identification with the poetics of math is evident in the three techniques that he uses to generate material forms.

The first way is taking tectonic elements and using them in extreme conditions. Bordeaux Villa is a good example, where the table configuration was transformed. I think the Villa Savoy was a moment of

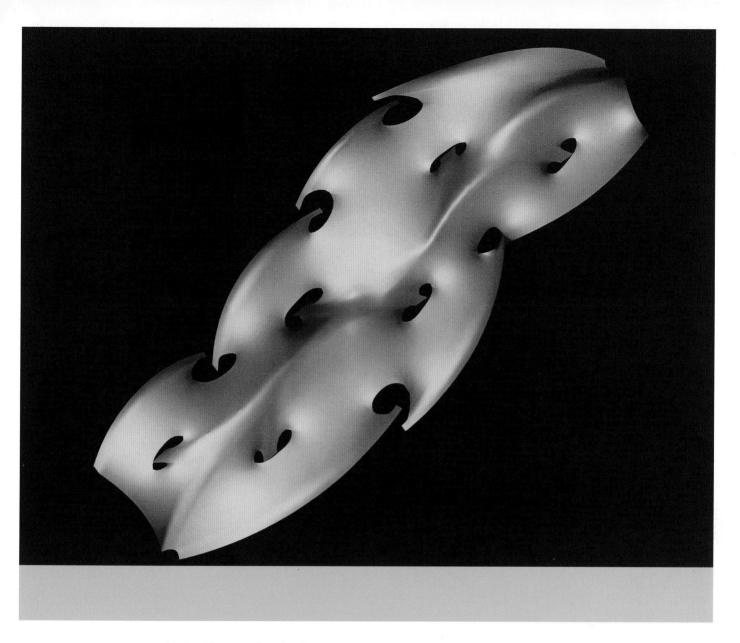

Notes
1. *Number 9* is a study on the hidden patterns behind our decimal system.
2. The first mandala is a symmetric Ptolemaic Universe of numbers held in concentric circles. The second mandala is a figure of eight orbits in different amplitudes converging and crisscrossing at one point – this is a transformation of the first, closed and symmetric mandala into the contemporary action, similar to that of a strange attractor.

perfection. The paradigm is of a secure mass supported off the ground symmetrically, and the mnemanic is temple. Such icons of architecture, exert a paralysis on the mind and make it difficult to investigate new forms. Koolhaas challenged me, saying, "Let's make the box fly." Bordeaux is a simple movement of columns in space – there are two skewed movements, in plan and in elevation. That simple shift and break with symmetry created the energy we wanted and a sense of momentum is gained.'

The second way is the generative line. I take a line and propel it through space in three dimensions. That has led to interesting forms. It is essentially a geometrical algorithm, and there is a rigour to the rules. But occasionally the movement of the line itself can be free, for example in the Chavasse Park project I worked on with Philip Johnson and Studio Baad. In this method materiality comes immediately after the concept algorithm, rapidly modifying the three-dimensional trajectory. It is not a simple sequence, but rather a constant interchange between concept and materiality as the work unfolds.

The third method is far more speculative, but potentially very rich. I work with grid points in space, and each point carries information. This is not information in a Cartesian sense, of location in relation to the x, y and z axes, but rather information about how the points relate to their neighbours within a set of prescribed rules. All that you need is one move. It forces one to think 'highly local' and to find one move in space, and to use overlap and feedback to extrapolate form. My studios at Harvard and Yale are based on this process. This work awaits a detailed articulation, which I hope to publish later.'

Informal is to be published in January 2002. The book covers case studies of the projects, and an expose of Cecil Balmond's use of the word 'informal', used for the first time at a lecture in 1991 in Berlin. The processes he is advocating in structure are integrative, and lead to notions of slip, jump, overlap, wrap and aggregate. *Informal* sets out a clear description of the long engagement with the nonlinear techniques that he has worked with, and the built and unbuilt results of those techniques (from Bordeaux to Arnhem). It is a book about his work, his theory and an explanation of his thoughts in developing that work. Δ

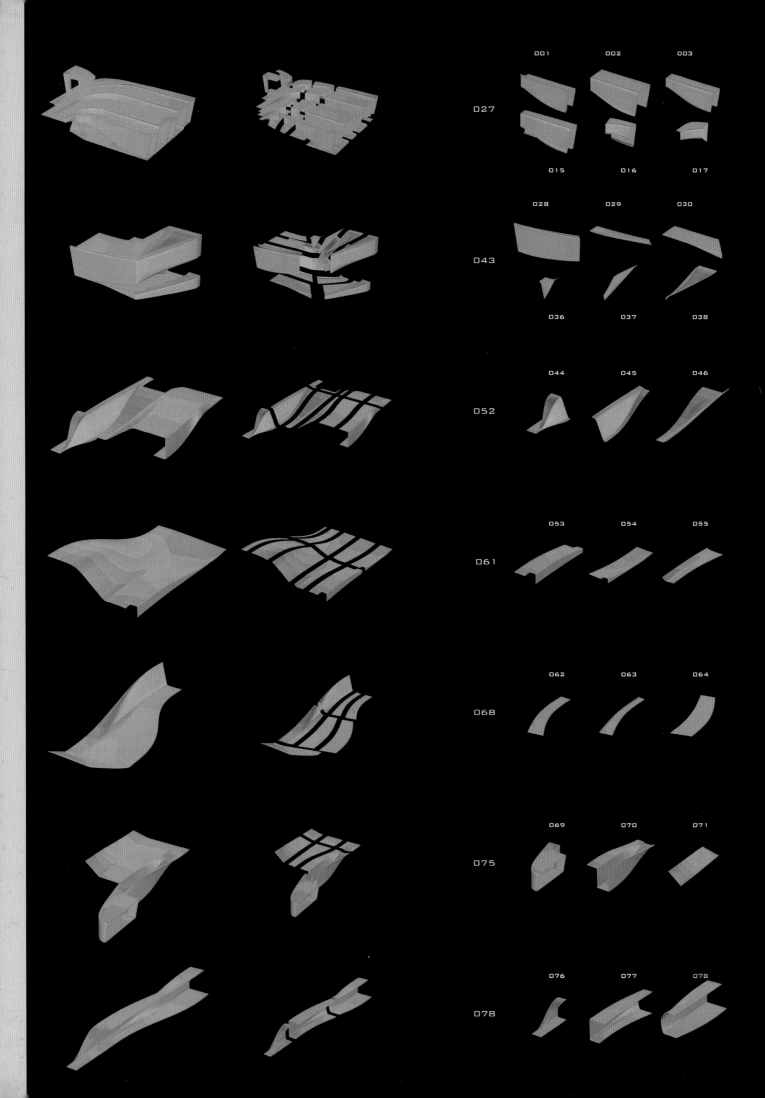

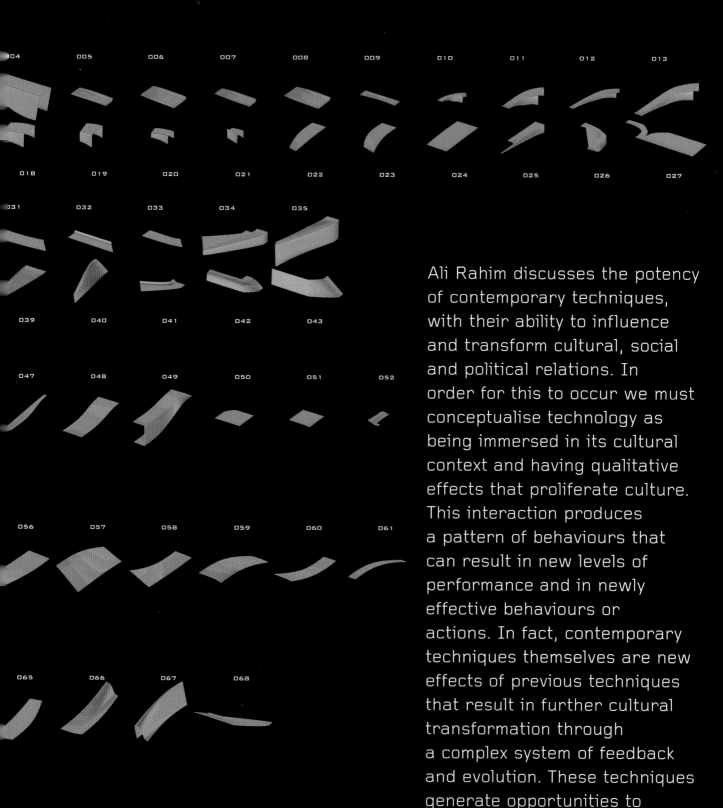

Ali Rahim discusses the potency of contemporary techniques, with their ability to influence and transform cultural, social and political relations. In order for this to occur we must conceptualise technology as being immersed in its cultural context and having qualitative effects that proliferate culture. This interaction produces a pattern of behaviours that can result in new levels of performance and in newly effective behaviours or actions. In fact, contemporary techniques themselves are new effects of previous techniques that result in further cultural transformation through a complex system of feedback and evolution. These techniques generate opportunities to produce new effects at the scale of organisation, programme, space and material.

Potential Performative Effects

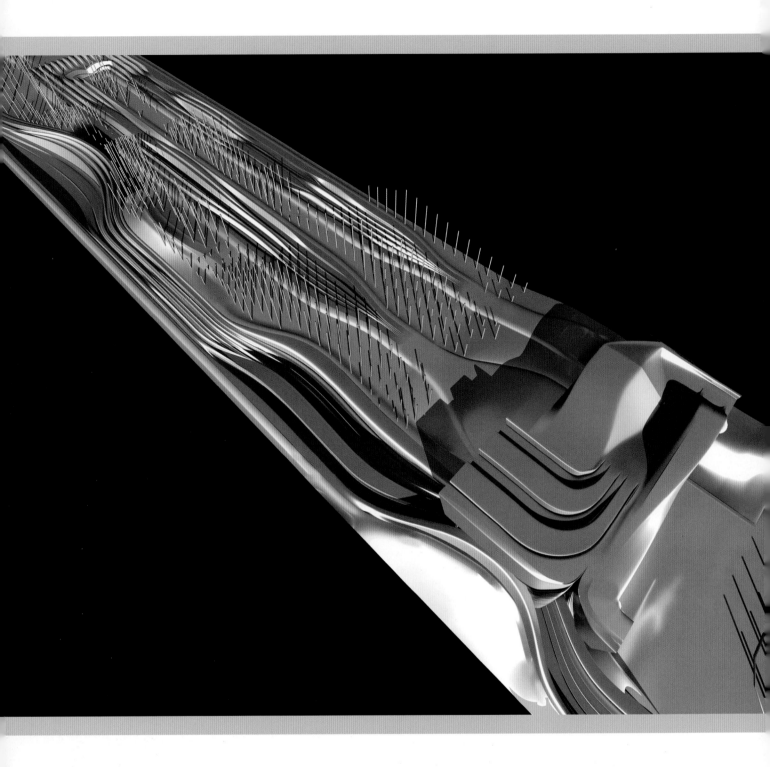

Contemporary design techniques are temporal, process-driven methods that provide new transformative effects in cultural, social and political production. Such a technique acts on or influences an object, which in turn modifies human behaviours and technical performance. Techniques have always contributed to the production of human and cultural artefacts, but their refinement and acceleration after the Industrial Revolution has emerged as the single most important element in the evolution of cultural endeavours.[1] Our work seeks to harness the potential of contemporary techniques to produce new architectural effects.

At each stage in its development, a technological device expresses a range of meanings not from 'technical rationality' but from the past practices of users. In this way a feedback loop is established between technology and cultural production that leads to a restless proliferation of new effects. That is, technology is not merely technical; it is an active and transformative entity resulting in new and different cultural effects.[2] Technology, in this sense, is not efficiency-oriented practice measured by quantities but a qualitative set of relations that interact with cultural stimuli. This interaction produces a pattern of behaviours that can result in new levels of performance and in newly effective behaviours or actions. In fact, contemporary techniques are themselves new effects of previous techniques and result in further cultural transformation through a complex system of feedback and evolution. The path of evolution produced by a cultural entity – an object, a building, a company or a career immersed in its context – produces a distinct lineage[3] as the result of propagation. Each lineage – economic, political, social, commercial, scientific, technological, etc – exists indefinitely through time, either in the same or an altered state. Time is qualitative in that the past, present and the future are simultaneous and contain maximum potential for optimising the capacity to grow, develop and come into being. The future is undecided, is bound by its past and is accretive. This allows us to be opportunistic with the potential for maximising new effects. Contemporary techniques enable us to access these potentials and separate these lineages. This act of separation is similar to propagation, producing a performative effect.

Once lineages have produced effects memes provide for the dissemination of ideas that cross these lineages. Memes are copied behaviours and are transmitted either through people by

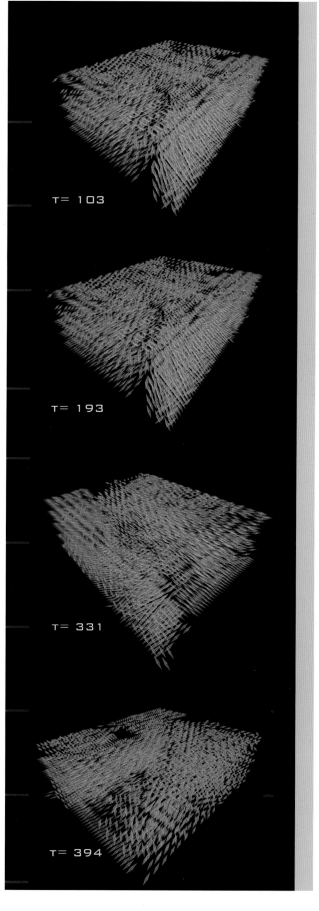

T= 103

T= 193

T= 331

T= 394

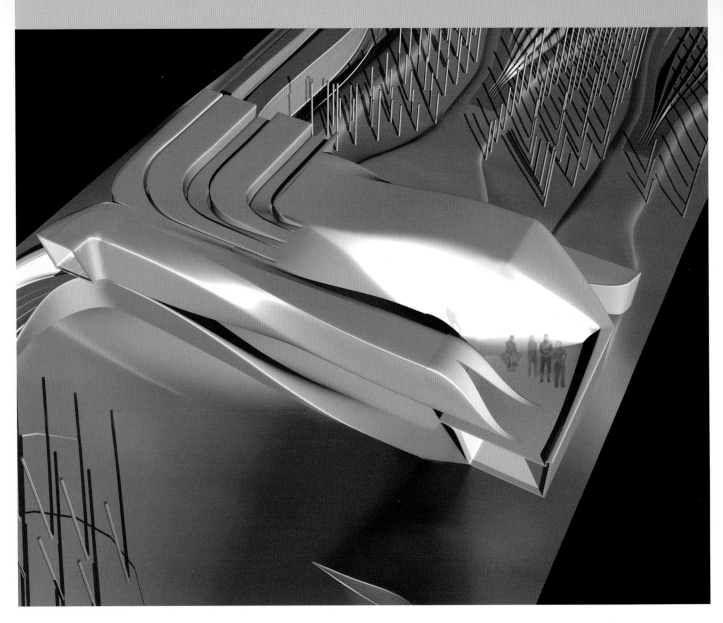

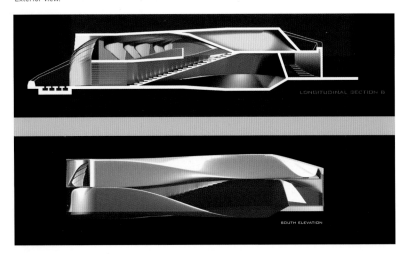

LONGITUDINAL SECTION B

SOUTH ELEVATION

heredity, in which the form and details of behaviours are copied; through variation, in which the behaviours are copied with errors; and through selection, in which only some behaviours are successfully copied. They react to external stimuli and produce or transform a situation through influence and effect. They are performative. To quote Stephen J Gould, '... transmission across lineages is, perhaps, the major source of cultural change.'[4]

For example, in the evolution of the computer, it is clear that each lineage encompasses the contributions of scholars, philosophers, visionaries, inventors, engineers, mathematicians, physicists and technicians. Each lineage was stimulated over time by vision, need, experience, competence and competition. As these lineages developed simultaneously through time, philosophically and intellectually they organised effects already in existence – the use of machines and automation. Theoretically they organised advances made in symbolic logic and science mathematics, which only then became feasible. These factors, impacted by differing intensities of economic, commercial, scientific, political and military pressures, crossed the technical threshold and spontaneously emerged into the technological object of the computer – an effect.

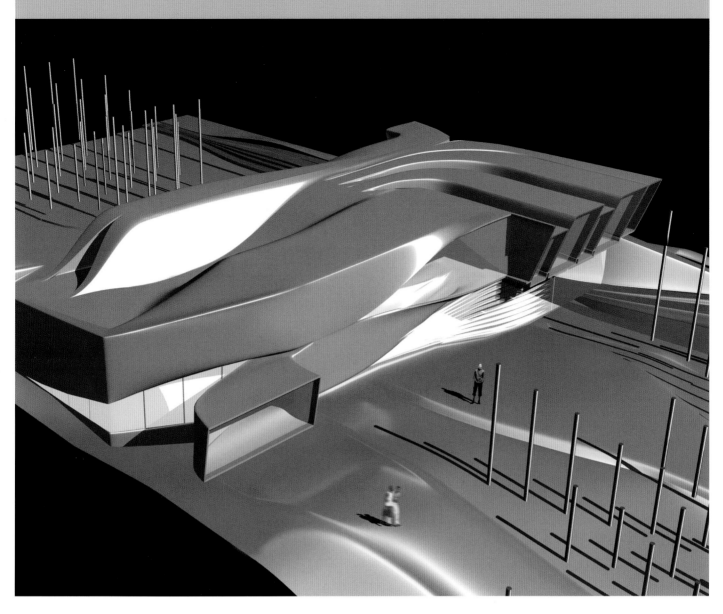

The computer is a temporally organised technological object. If we were to view these nonlinear organisational processes as fixed in space and time, the resulting objects would be severely limited and would strain to represent meaning through formal expression. This object type would be passive and defined only by its material attributes, which are linear and causal. Such an object is static, and only has the capacity to produce predetermined effects.

To avoid this stasis, we must view the object in its context, and understand it as part of a continuous temporal organisational process of cultural proliferation. This process is endogenic, machinic and has the potential to spontaneously self-assemble, and produce effects that are qualitative and larger than initially anticipated. The effects – no longer proportional to their causes – are emergent. For example, the Internet was initially created for the purpose of exchanging information between nuclear facilities operated by the military. However, it has emerged as the largest storage bank of information in the world with far greater and more complex performative potential than could ever have been predicted. Once recontextualised, the computer is instrumental in spreading memes, which change behaviours and continue to influence contemporary culture.

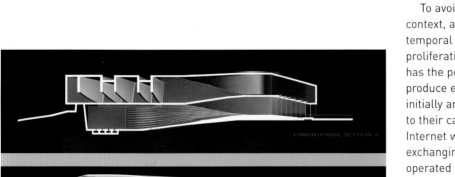

LONGITUDINAL SECTION A

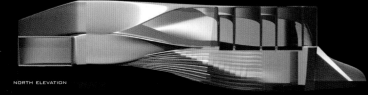

NORTH ELEVATION

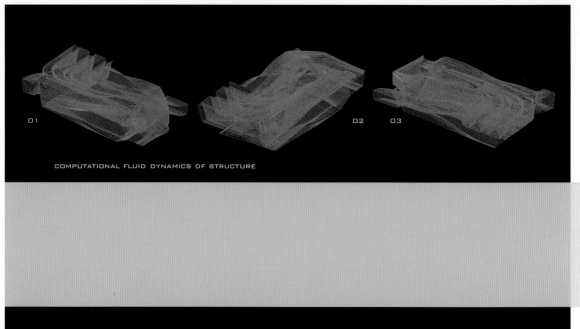

COMPUTATIONAL FLUID DYNAMICS OF STRUCTURE

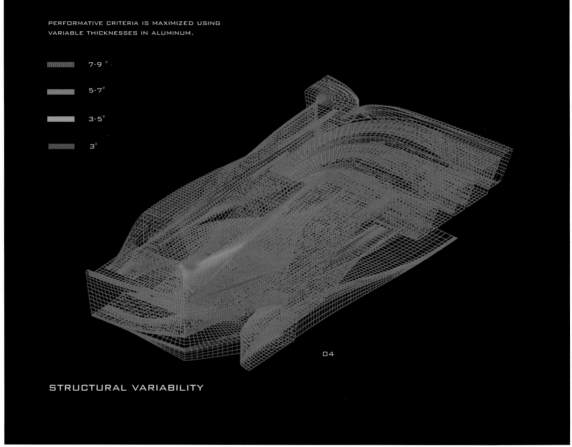

PERFORMATIVE CRITERIA IS MAXIMIZED USING
VARIABLE THICKNESSES IN ALUMINUM.

7-9"

5-7"

3-5"

3"

STRUCTURAL VARIABILITY

Contemporary techniques are organised and guided by probabilities, which are unlimited and allow for the production of performative effects in architecture. Moreover, contemporary techniques are destabilised by temporally located potentials that make possible the development of new organisations. These processes amplify the difference between the possible and the real, and contain a set of possibilities which acquire physical reality as resemblant material form. The static object that produces predetermined effects defines the real, whereas contemporary processes allow for exploration of the possibilities. Actualisation, on the other hand, is emergent and breaks with

resemblant materiality bringing to the fore a new sensibility, which ensures that the difference between the real and actual is always a genuine creation.[5] This sensibility, which subverts fixed identity, is a flexible spatiotemporal organisation that produces performative effects. Its effectiveness is measured by the capacity to produce new effects. This is tested through an iterative process where the possibilities become genuinely open-ended.

In order to fully maximise the potential provided by contemporary techniques, we use machinic, nonlinear techniques within time-based software where time is irreversible. This software simulates the natural processes of contemporary cultural production, whereby the past and present are simultaneous and the

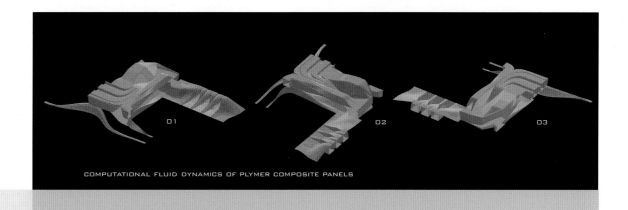

COMPUTATIONAL FLUID DYNAMICS OF PLYMER COMPOSITE PANELS

01　　　　02　　　　03

PERFORMATIVE CREITERIA IS MAXIMIZED IN POLYMER
COMPOSITE PANLES BY VARIED THICKNESSES.

3"

1-3"

0.5"-1"

0.5"

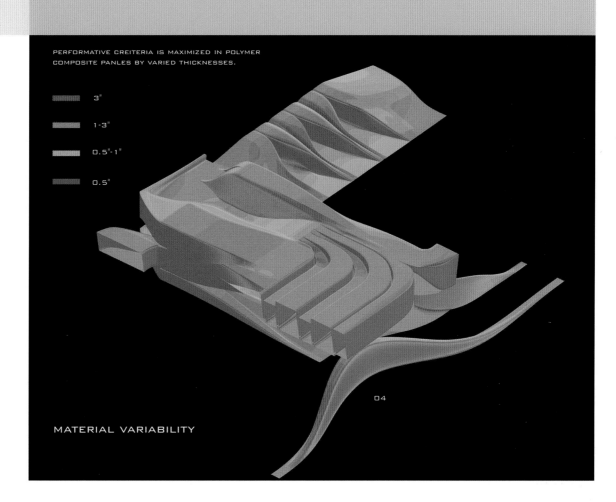

04

MATERIAL VARIABILITY

future is not preconceived.[6] Our intention in architectural projects is to actualise virtualities contained within the matrices of the software that fully exploit its potential to produce new effects, which modify behaviours and performance.

This process of actualisation allows us to produce temporal organisations through an iterative process that is conditioned by our ideas and concepts. There is a continuous feedback loop within the context of this ongoing investigation. This working method allows us to shape and tune the formations in accordance with our concepts through a process of actualisation.[7] Knowledge and sensibility are

produced at all developmental stages within the project, the effects of which are organisational, programmatic, spatial and material. One possibility out of many is actualised. Through interaction with the environment our creations transform cultural production. This is an ongoing temporal process of cultural proliferation which self-perpetuates.

In our project for Variations, a residence in Islamabad, Pakistan, we conceptualised an approach that locally affiliated site, organisation, programme, space and material challenges. The form of the project emerged from spatial considerations that influenced all scales of development. This was developed through the study of the site in addition to the intensive schedule of events that it would be necessary to

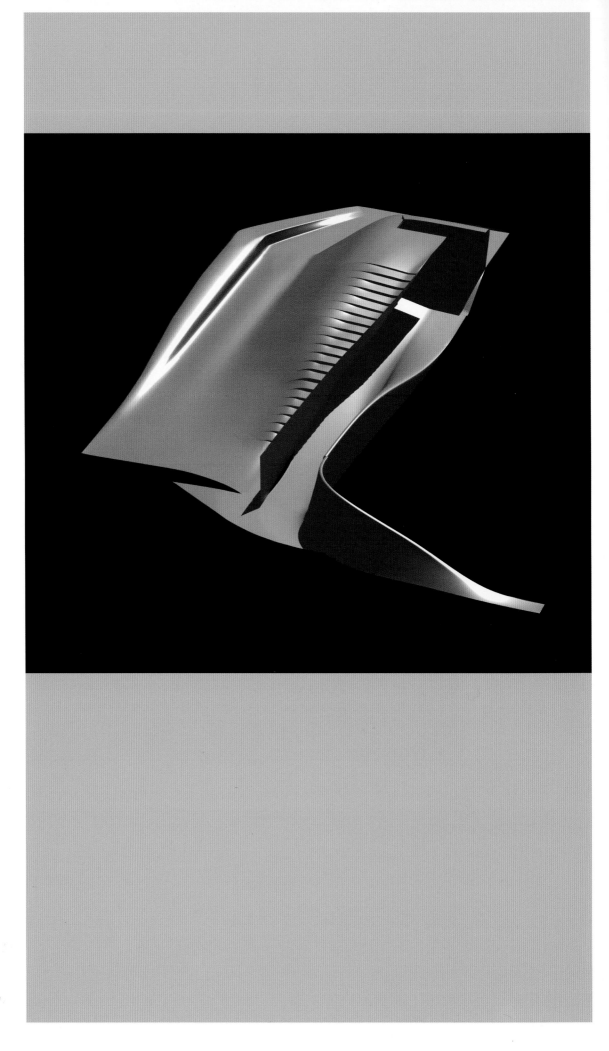

Right
Interior view of the main
circulation spaces showing
that it is possible for multiple
event intensities to occur
simultaneously.

contain within the landscape and inhabitation of the project. We used animation techniques that evolved through time to study the relationship of the scale and intensity of events and their correspondences with the temporal cycles of the site. Specifically, we used inverse kinematics, which coded events as a field condition, and which had an equal capacity to react to particular site cycles measured by their intensity, duration and frequency. These relationships were deterritorialised through the use of vectorial and gradient force fields that responded to different degrees of environmental specificity. For example an existing well on the site was coded with a continuous pointal force which acted on the field condition, and subsequently reacted to the continuous vector of force exerted on it. This provided unlimited potential in the system which grew in complexity, evolved and formed mutual associations between site stimuli and event. These pointed towards future possibilities, and were guided and shaped to form tendencies through an iterative process.

The actualisation process involved applying these tendencies to multiplicities in event intensity and duration, producing a variety of performative effects. A system of differentiated channels modulating water flow was actualised to provide for drainage and irrigation during different seasons. That is, a system of troughs and channels is used to irrigate or drain the land

Below
Cross section

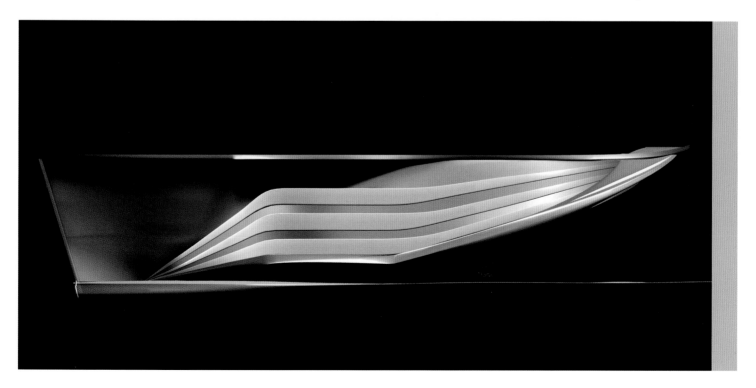

61

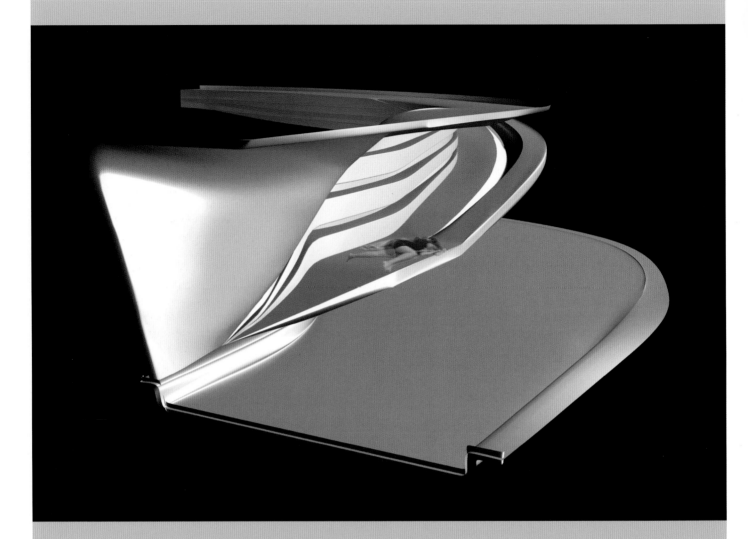

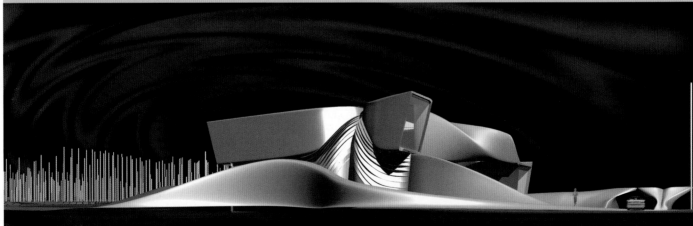

Above
Secondary circulation path
allows for abrupt stoppages
of space, providing for unseen
events.

Below
Overall view showing the
gradient effects of light.

PERSPECTIVE VIEW

Notes
1. Larry A Hickman, *Philosophical Tools for Technological Culture. Putting pragmatism to work*, Indiana University Press (Bloomington), 2001.
2. Andrew Feenberg, *Putting Pragmatism to work: Questioning technology*, Routledge (London and New York), 1999. Feenberg describes how the invariant elements of the constitution of the technical subject and object become modified, socially specific contextualising variables in the course of the realisation of concrete technical actors, devices and systems. Thus technologies are not merely efficient devices, or efficiency-oriented practices, but include contexts as these are embodied in design and social insertion.
3. A lineage is the evolutionary path demarcated by a single cultural entity, or combination of cultural entities, through time as the result of replication.
4. Stephen J Gould, *Bully for Brontosaurus*, Norton (New York), 1991, p 65.
5. Gilles Deleuze, *Difference and Repetition* (European Perspectives: A Series in Social Thought and Cultural Criticism), trans Paul Patton, Columbia University Press (New York), 1994.
6. This is constructive. For further discussion, see 'Systemic Delay – Breaking the Mould', *Architectural Design* Vol 70, No 3, June 2000, p6.
7. The idea comes from the French philosopher Henri Bergson who, at the turn of the century, wrote a series of texts in which he criticised the inability of the science of his time to think the new, the truly novel. According to Bergson the first obstacle was a mechanical and linear view of causality and the rigid determinism it implied. Clearly, if all the future is already given in the past, if the future is merely that modality of time where previously determined possibilities become realised, then true innovation is impossible.

providing a contingency of effects according to ecological specificity. Ecologically, the effects are controlled to develop through time. For example, localised effects are produced by regulating the direction, amount, drainage and flow of water within the system at any given time. This controls not only the scale and type of vegetation, but also the activities surrounding the system. Water is collected or released according to differing levels of saturation. A pool for swimming in summer becomes a retention pond in winter. This provides for a matrix of possibilities coded into a flexible yet specific organisation of water channels. These channels combine to form an emergent organisation of water flow that produces programmatic, material and ecological effects that influence behaviours.

At the scale of habitation we see a continuity with the landscape where the actualised organisational process has no bounded limits – figure or ground, building or landscape, inside or outside, public or private – but provides a continuous interchange or gradient between the two extremes. This allows for the maximum variety of effective scenarios to occur which merge programmatic events. Different alternative scales of circulation routes through the organisation are used and activated at different times during the day, week and year, producing markedly different effects. For example, the main circulation route provides for multiple events, while the short-cuts of secondary and tertiary scale provide for connections that can collapse two simultaneous events. This continuous differentiation of porosity determines various performative effects at different times during the project. For example, if two events of the same intensity simultaneously occur – dining on the first and second levels – they are joined by the secondary or tertiary scales of circulation, merging with each other. If they are two separate events with different intensities, for example dining and entertaining, they spawn additional unforeseen events.

Spaces are arranged by a more detailed set of performative possibilities. One location may provide for clustering and accumulative behaviour, while another allows for ease of dispersion and continuity of space. For example, while entertaining one is able to flow seamlessly from one space to another. In other instances the space acts as a resistance to disrupt the flow. This disruption causes unforeseen situations to occur. In addition, spaces are modulated by the

ransformation of surface specificity which allows for various functions: sitting, eating, sleeping, bathing. For example, seating, which may also be used for sleeping, transforms into leaning spaces, which can become areas for social interaction. This gives the opportunity for that particular use, or the space can be reappropriated for various uses in various combinations.

Within system, surface and space, material is modulated at the molecular level and at the scale of enclosure. At the molecular level, continuous variation is possible within nonisotropic (composite) materials; densities or porosities provide a range of gradient effects. The threshold of the line is moved to a gradient so that opaque, translucent and transparent effects can occur in one surface in continuous variation. This rearticulates the intention to conflate the internal spatial effects while simultaneously producing aesthetic effects of various transparencies and colours. At the scale of enclosure one can vary the thickness of the surface, dependent on its own material logic, for strength and for levels of opacity. By twisting the material one is able to produce a range of lighting effects.

The emerged organisation is made of an aluminum structure, which is draped with composite materials that range from opaque to transparent in appearance. This relies on the technological and material manufacturing capability of contemporary culture, that of the aeroplane, which has been recontextualised to produce new architectural effects.

Spaces are arranged by a more detailed set of performative possibilities. One location may provide for clustering and accumulative behaviour, while another allows for ease of dispersion and continuity of space.

The structure develops through the process simultaneously with its material counterpart, and affiliates itself with varying levels of porosity. This aligns different densities of structure with different intensities of programme. In the process, the structure is decoded and freed from dependency on pointal load transference to one determined by difference in load-bearing pressures. It provides for an open organisation which is specific while simultaneously producing another layer of ambient effects. This potential, when combined with differing densities of composite material panels, provides for a series of emergent lighting effects. This spatiotemporal organisation is performative, and seeks variability at all scales – within programme, space, structure and material. ⌂

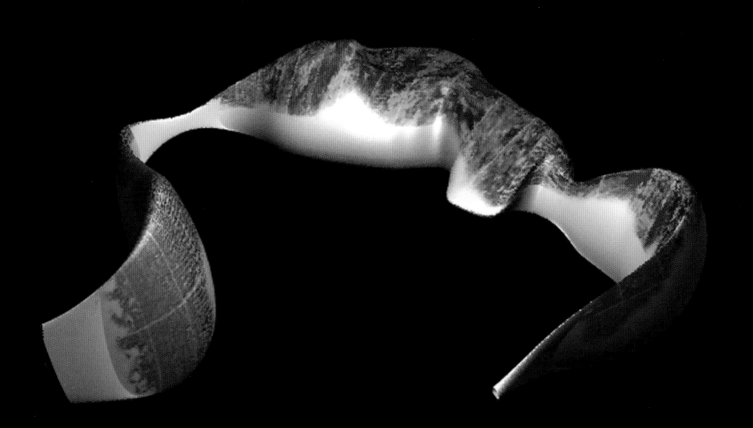

Predator

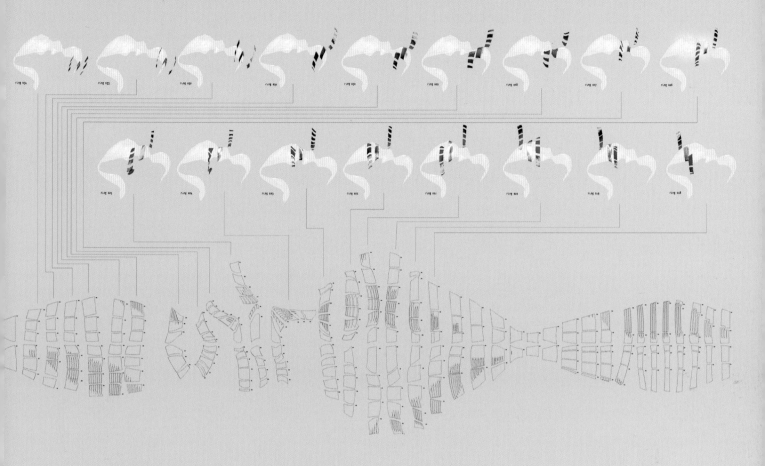

The new sensibility brought about through contemporary techniques uses geometric ambiguity, new composite forms and their occupants, providing for mixtures of different programmes, spaces and materials to organise experiences that affect the subject. **Greg Lynn** in *Predator*, an installation exhibited at the Wexner Center in Columbus, Ohio (27 January – 15 April 2001) creates varying scales of spatial, material and ambient effects, through the use of shredded vacu-formed moulds engulfed in a painting by Fabian Marcaccio. This new sensibility that emerges blurs inside with outside and top with bottom. The experience is enhanced by the lighting patterns that are transmitted through the different shredded openings and the translucent painting by Marcaccio.

Greg Lynn's collaboration with Fabian Marcaccio for the *Predator*, a 30-foot-wide, 10-foot-high vacuformed and painted plastic structure, is a voluptuous painting/architecture mutant hybrid. It explores the potentiality contained within the multiplicity of conceptual and manufacturing techniques that give rise to various digital techniques for the design and fabrication of architectural and industrial design objects. The alien organism as architecture was designed digitally with animation software which produced many variations prior to the actualisation of a specific form. The actualised form snakes through the Wexner Center in Columbus, Ohio, distorting the spatiality of the museum while putting emphasis on a series of new effects at many scales.

The effects include the transparency of the vacuformed panels covered with laser-printed images of the original painting by Fabian, and an additional layer of paint to add yet another level of colour, texture and scale. These produce different degrees of lighting quality when the viewer moves around or through the object. The vacuformed surfaces are thin with a series of shreds at various scales that allow new lighting effects to enter the spatiality.

The effects are simultaneously generated by silk-screening and painting vacuformed plastic, using very specific digital techniques and methods to wrap a continuously differentiated form in a continuous flat surface. Each panel is different in size, and has different degrees of curvature dependent on the limitations of the milling machine and the size of the 4 × 8 foot MDF panels, which are held together by three-dimensional plates manufactured using a 3-axis computer numerically controlled (CNC) router.

The types of material exhibited in Form's project include intricate miniature models built of light-sensitive resin hardened with a computer-controlled laser beam (stereolithography process); coloured eurethane models cast into silicon forms; and three-dimensionally shaped aluminium plates manufactured using a computer-controlled carving tool (3-axis CNC router). ⊅

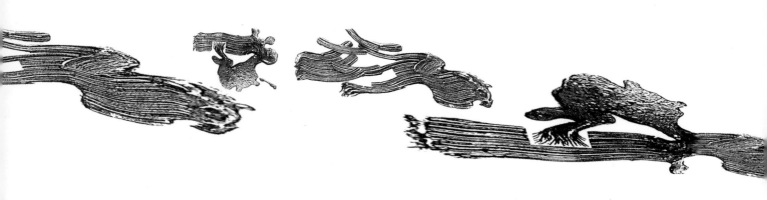

Previous spread right
The process of converting the
complex variegated form into
discrete rings formulates the
logic of connection from one
panel to another. The panels are
of different sizes and curvatures.
The degree of curvature is
limited to the maximum
thickness the machine can mill.

Above
Fabian Marcaccio's original
painting which determined a
series of relationships, and
animated and posited a series
of different effects.

Right (detail previous spread left)
Fabian's painting in black
and white was used as a
displacement map to generate
ideas for different shreds and
textures.

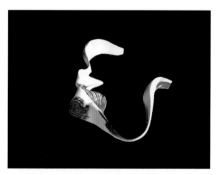

Opposite
The textures are mapped on
to the surface of the project
resulting in a series of
deformations due to its
curvature.

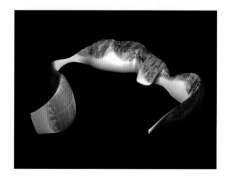

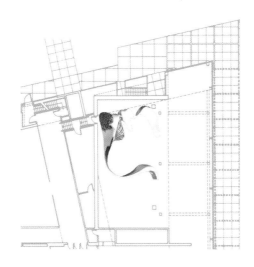

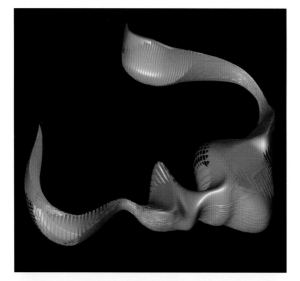

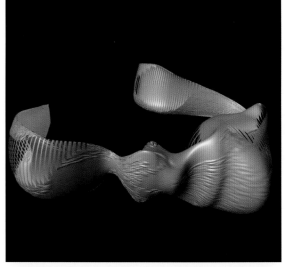

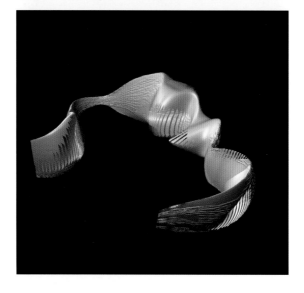

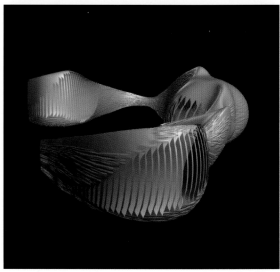

Above
Image of the floor plan of the Wexner Center, with *Predator*.

Right
The displacements were mapped on to the surface, revealing the texture of the original brush strokes.

Opposite
The final form of all the vacuformed panels.

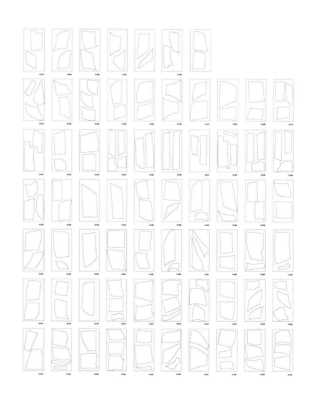

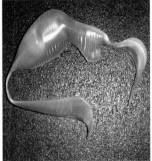

Above
The final form of the miniature stereolithography model built from light-sensitive resin hardened with a computer-controlled laser beam.

Above and below
The process of determining the mapped painting on to each surface.

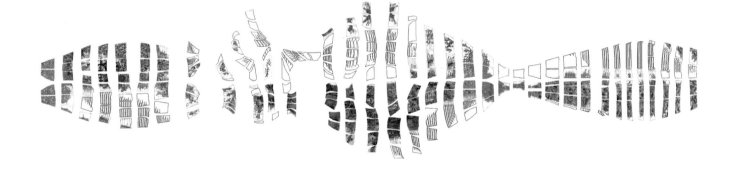

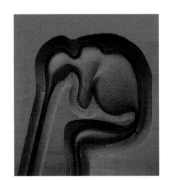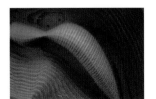

Right (left to right)
Milled-wood models, made using a 3-axis CNC milling machine, describe the form of the project.

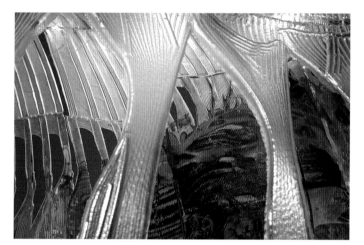

Above top left
Overall view of *Predator* in the exhibition space of the Wexner Center, revealing the transformation of space through different effects.

Above top right
Interior view of the *Predator*.

Above left and right
Interior views of *Predator* showing the effects of the shredded vacuformed surfaces and their textures – in addition to being silk-screened they are layered with textured paint.

Right
Interior view showing the connections between the various sizes of panels.

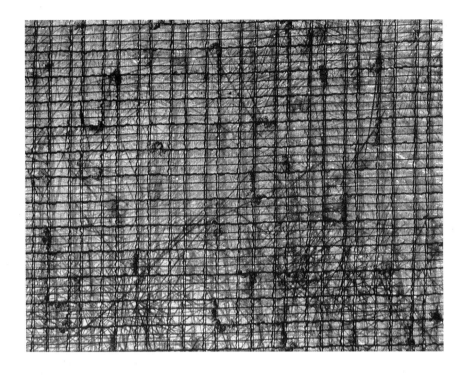

Skin Deep

Polymer Composite Materials in Architecture

Johan Bettum is the leader of the Polymer Composite Materials in Architecture (PCMA) research programme at the Oslo School of Architecture, Norway. Here he describes the newly discovered potential of polymer composite materials to produce new aesthetic and spatial effects. Particularly useful for their time-conditioned, non-linear behaviours, polmer composites correspond with recent trends toward a temporal process-based approach to surfaces and a consequent focus on materials and material technologies. This approach centres on the possibilities and resistance of the surface as a 3-dimesnional entity. Moreover, Bettum's PCMA projects demonstrate the meaningful and dynamic role that articulation of surfaces can play in mass-cultural formation.

Above
Material test image, see p. 75

Right
Outside view towards service
area above entrance for the
Holiday Inn Express Hotel,
Sandefjord International
Airport, Norway, 1998–2001.

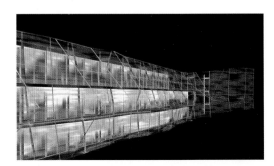

... The sea was indistinguishable from the sky, except that the sea was slightly creased as if a cloth had wrinkles on it. Gradually as the sky whitened a dark line lay on the northern horizon dividing the sea from the sky and the grey cloth became barred with thick strokes moving, one after the other, beneath the surface, following each other, pursuing each other, perceptually.

Virginia Woolf, *The Waves*, The Hogarth Press, (London), 1990, p1.

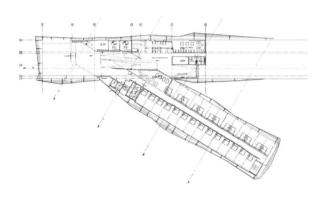

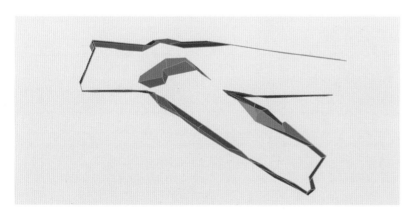

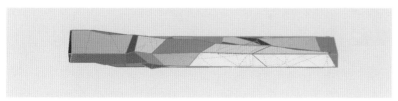

Above
Plan and models of the Holiday Inn Express Hotel, Sandefjord, showing geometry of outer envelope.

Surface Articulation

After nearly a decade of extensive interest in the potential of surface transformations to generate particular spatial organisations and typologies, a shift of focus is under way in architectural discourse and practice. This shift is directed away from treating surfaces as topological – accompanied by a methodological interest in the topographic (evident in numerous projects over the last few years) – to a temporally conditioned articulation of surfaces. The shift is symptomatic of several tendencies in contemporary architecture and a direct extension and development of the aforementioned surface strategies.

The focus on surface articulation is fundamentally linked to, even uniquely expressed as, a corresponding interest in materials and material technology. Industrial improvements have fed a renewed preoccupation with materials' capacity to produce various aesthetic and spatial effects. The developments are facilitated in part by computers, some of which, in turn, become economically available for use in buildings.

In contrast to approaches based on types of topology or topography, current concerns with surface articulation are subject to the possibilities and resistances of the surface as a three-dimensional material entity. The surface must therefore be conceptualised and designed with respect to its depth. One must also consider its geometry, material make-up and composition of elements on a microscale, as well as the sectional definition of the envelope on a macroscale. This marks a difference from the traditional way of conceptualising the spatial perimeter, and requires us to rethink the dichotomies that have been inferred between structure and form, and structure and ornament. With surface articulation and its potential to engender a specific architectural performance, the focus is on the capacity of the surface to act as a filter in the production of architectural effects.

While the design process poses a challenge to the incorporation of new variables, there exists a concomitant need to theorise the ensuing dynamics that a capacitated surface stages. Traditional tectonic theory does not satisfactorily account for material systems, such as those addressed here, with high degrees of embedded heterogeneity and varied relationships to changing external conditions.

Our need is to reconceptualise the surface with respect to its material basis and manifestation. To paraphrase Janet Ward from her study of urban visual culture in 1920s Germany: we turn from our technologised surface culture to look not for metaphysical origins but for how surface plays a different, more dynamic, meaningful role in architectural formation. A current research project in Norway, *Polymer and Composite Materials in*

Architecture (PCMA) attempts to contribute to this development. The project is based on the nature and potential of these materials to provide an alternative resource to the traditional material spectrum for the production of architecture.

Matter of Fact

PCMA focuses on the design, construction and performance of the building envelope with this category of materials. Research topics include modulated light transmission, flexible modular production of building panels and systems, texturing and patterning of facade panels, construction strategies and mounting systems, and, finally, digital design processing – including modelling and performance analyses.

'Polymer composite materials', a contemporary and more specific term for the older 'plastic materials', suffer from having been regarded as a secondary, low-grade building material. While this was partly justified due to their relatively poor industrial quality and weathering capability in the 1960s and 1970s, it

theoretical framework. But it is significant in cultural terms, and polymer composite materials can be conceptually related to significant but frequently ignored architectural ideas – notably those of Gottfried Semper, and his theory of dressing based on textiles and the human impulse for decoration.

Meanwhile our culture is saturated with the pleasure, nuisance and promise of plastics. They define the entire consumer culture in which we are ensconced. Since the first house was constructed predominantly from polymer composites – Ionel Schein and colleagues' Snail House for the Paris Exhibition of 1955 – we can trace a line through OMA's use of polyester panels for the Congrexpo in Lille in 1990–94, via the proliferation of synthetic materials in a great number of more recent architectural projects, to the sanctification of plastics in the recent display in Milan of research by OMA and Herzog & de Meuron for their Prada shop projects. In light of this, one can wonder if it is not the regimes of theory and educational institutions, and the general conservatism of architecture as a whole, that has propagated an exclusion of these materials – culturally, practically and conceptually. The altogether

Below
Finite element analysis performed on the outer skin of a typical wall section for the Holiday Inn Express Hotel, Sndefjord. The analysis conducted simulated a minor wind load directedorthogonally on the façade. The mesh can be modified in order to optimise the precision and performance of the analysis.

Below left
Catia model: wall section with double skin & interstitial space. The inner façade is made of glass; the outer is made from flat polymer composite wall panels attached to a steel frame. Display of how wall panels were constrained during analysis: the wall panels are fastened in the model according to the design solution for the panel attachments.

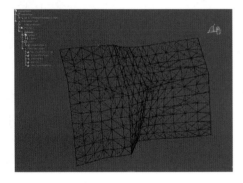  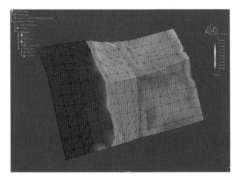

Above middle
Display of localised stress distribution in the façade panels based on von Mises' criteria The highest amount of stress is displayed as red. Depending on material tolerances, the analysis will indicate where the design needs to be modified.

Above right
Display of topographic deformation according to applied wind load.

means that current standards and practice with these materials are underdeveloped relative to those for aluminium and glass, for instance.

Polymer composite materials are of interest to architects since they have a relatively high strength-to-weight ratio compared to many others, represent a vast potential for producing novel aesthetic effects, are highly mouldable and require minimal maintenance. Greatly improved industrial material qualities compared to those 30 to 40 years ago, and more competitive prices, imply that polymer composite materials have come of age.

In modern industrial terms, the materials are not 'new' but are about half a century old. This is a negligible history compared to the more than two millennia during which stone, wood, brick, iron, steel and glass have supplied the material and epistemological basis for architecture, and a continuum for developing a practical and

'otherness' of polymer and composite materials, despite Sigfried Giedion's embrace of the latter's value for architecture, means that we often lack the means to comprehend the possibilities that these materials offer. To fully explore their practical implications we need to know more precisely what polymer and composite materials actually consist of.

A composite is a solid material that is obtained when two or more different constituent material elements, each with its own characteristics, are mixed. The result is a new substance whose properties are different and superior to those of the original elements but where the mixed elements retain their individual characteristics. In practice, a composite is usually a combination of two principal elements: reinforcement and matrix. While there are different ways to categorise industrial composites, there are principally three major groups, each named according to the matrix material: metal matrix composites (MMC), ceramic matrix composites (CMC) and polymer matrix composite (PMC). The last is

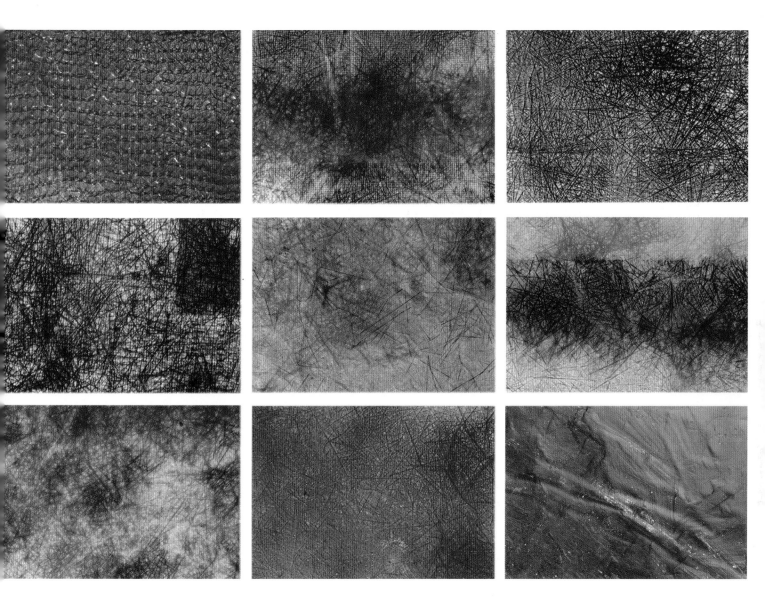

Above
Material tests exploring
different graphic patterns
and degrees of light
transmission resulting from
a clear polyester and various
reinforcement and
additives. Material elements
used include: transparent
polyester, different
mixes of woven polyester
mesh, chopped glassfibre
rovings, glassfibre mats,
paper and colour additives.

termed polymer because the matrix is made from substances that consist of giant molecules formed from smaller molecules of the same substance. Typical matrix materials for architectural PMCs are polyester and epoxy.

The reinforcement, such as fibres of one or another kind and type, is embedded in the matrix which acts as an adhesive. In addition to the two principal elements, reinforcement and matrix, a composite can also contain additives and fillers. The latter are often employed to add volume with minimal weight gain. The former can be chemical compounds that yield, for instance, colour or improve fire performance. While additives and fillers can influence the strength of the composite, it is primarily the choice of matrix and reinforcement, and the interface between these, that determines the properties and performance capabilites of the product.

There are a number of different kinds of fibre,

both inorganic and organic: glass, carbon, aramide and polyethylene, to mention some. These come in a variety of different types, such as continuous or chopped roving, chopped strand mats and fabrics. Due to cost, glass fibre is the standard type of reinforcement in architecture. The most advanced fibre-based products are knitted and woven fabrics. Industrial knitting and weaving machines allow for an additional high degree of variability, including mixing different types of fibre. The result is a two- or three-dimensional arrangement that is based on the yarn's array of knots in the case of knitting, and a pattern of interlacing in the case of weaving.

Finally, there are numerous ways to produce the composite itself. It consists of layers of reinforcement that, through the action of the matrix material, are laminated on top of one another. A mould is needed even for a flat, open surface. The boatbuilding industry, which produces some of the largest, single-shell structures, is based on manual or half-automatic processes. For smaller scale products, for example in the automotive industry, the matrix material is transferred into a closed mould with the help of a partial vacuum and pressure. Facade panels are produced either with resin transfer moulding or continuous lamination processes on a rolling band.

In architecture most instances of PMC applications are based on standard, off-the-shelf building products, of which there are already a great number, from panels to standard profiles that correspond to standard steel sections. When examined on a macroscopic level, the use of such products seemingly complies with the tenure of established architectural theory and practice. In fact, in most instances of PMC applications, these materials directly substitute for conventional building materials. Architecture is then still based on the assumption that the materials are homogeneous, isotropic, without depth and that the structure behaves linearly – there is direct proportionality between stress and strain. It is a reality constructed on a Vitruvian model of proportionality and relative sameness. Space, whether inside or outside, supervenes material enclosure and is not the resultant gradient continuum of calibrated architectural systems of which the material is one.

The Matter of Synthesis

On a microscopic level, polymer composites are heterogeneous material systems where, for instance, the directionality of fibre reinforcement can be tailored to include local areas that absorb anticipated directional load both in 2-D and 3-D. The materials do not predate a given application, and their exact composition needs to be determined to meet with desired performance criteria. While this is a hypothetical situation in most instances of a contemporary, common building economy, it is nonetheless a defining criterion for polymer composites. Furthermore, optimising material choices and the composition of a composite allows for weight reduction and is an economical solution for extreme constructions where the time-conditioned nonlinear behaviour of composites can be utilised.

When it comes to other performance criteria, handling design and construction with polymer composites is a very complex task. In a unique, practical manner the very beginning of a design process is immediately connected to, and informed by, the desired result and its anticipated conditions. This situation poses organisational and logistic demands on the design process that completely overturn the traditional role of the architect. The distinction between quantitative and qualitative variables and considerations in the process from idea to final product can no longer be maintained. The task is then to handle the information flow not only to – but also actually within – the project. This internal coordination of goals, facts, designs and analyses includes aesthetic, material and general performance criteria. For example, form and structure are no longer categorically distinct but may flow in and out of one another.

The idea of relations in traditional tectonic theory cannot circumscribe the different levels of economy and variance that polymer composite materials introduce. These materials, like composites in general, introduce new aspects and entirely different types and scales of relations that rely on a new concept of informational flow through matter. In order to access, instrumentalise and optimise the synergy of these flows, the operational design strategy must maintain and join the disparate subchannels of matter and information that charge the project. This operation cannot seek compromises in a Hegelian sense of synthesis, but must subscribe to the idea of synthesis in the writings of Gilles Deleuze, where those things that are synthesised are negotiated, individually maintained, but never resolved.

The polymer composite surface is, coincidentally, itself a product of synthesis. Its promise for architecture is that it is beyond being treated in the diagrammatic manner of recent folding strategies. These have in effect considered the surface as an immaterial and pliable two-dimensional datum with no depth or internal structure, activated by the formal manipulation of the geometry and/or through the deployment of programmatic fields. They have consequently suppressed the essential material basis that is the origin of the diagrams and impeded further study of these phenomena in relation to architecture as a material practice. Beyond the face of it, surface organisation is returned to the surface and our task is to articulate it. ⊅

Below
View of polymer composite panel in its initial manifestation.

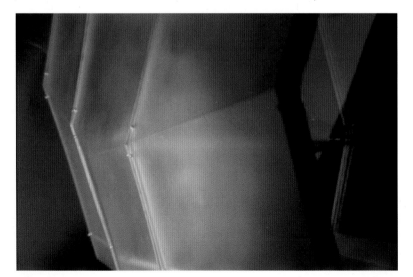

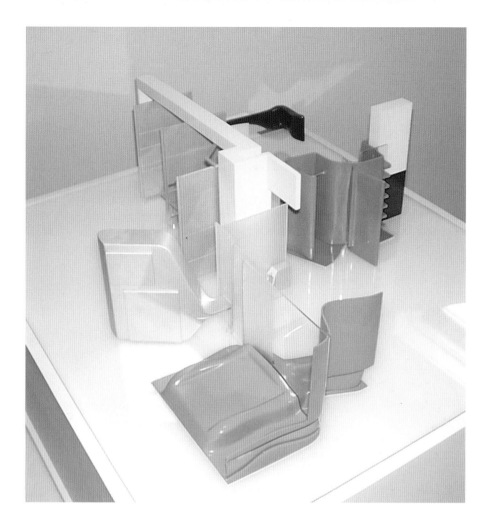

'Lumping'

Contemporary techniques can re-contextualise normative techniques to produce new architectural effects. For example, Kolatan/MacDonald Studio re-contextualise techniques used in the boat building industry, to vary and modulate the continuity of surface within their apartment renovation. **Sulan Kolatan** and **Bill MacDonald** explain how the effects of this modulation provide for new spatial articulation, where one continuous surface is moulded specifically for different uses, while still leaving the possibilities open for other unplanned events.

'Recently, while reading the "Science" section of the *New York Times,* I focused with relief on an article that discussed the basic activities of science with refreshing simplicity. It maintained that most scientists may be grouped into two categories: those who like to "lump" and those who like to "split". While apparently some degree of splitting is often inevitable for lumpers, as is some lumping for splitters, both groups are partial to their respective modes of operation. Thus, lumpers look for correspondences between seemingly unrelated things and phenomena, whereas splitters search for differences in things and phenomena which appear to be similar. After experiencing an immediate sense of recognition, followed by a sense of exhilaration about being able to name in precise scientific terms what I had been interested in pursuing for a while now albeit in the "House and Home" section of the *New York Times*. I was a "lumper" now, wasn't I?

Lumping Presupposes Lateral Operations
The logic of lumping, of bringing together different – sometimes disparate – elements, has to do with lateral

operations. Cross- and inter- are its prefixes, as in cross-breeding and interdependence, cross-section and interface, cross-category and interstice, cross-platforming and interdisciplinary. Lumping proliferates horizontally, by blending between already matured systems across different categories. The concept of lumping, as used in the aforementioned article, differs from the common use of the term in that it is not haphazard but, rather, significant and consequent. Significant lumping affords productive leaps – it has rules and consequent yields.

Let's take ferrofluids. If you merely lump shaved magnetite into oil – nothing happens. The fluid and magnetic substances act as if they were alone. If, however, you calibrate the shavings of magnetite to be about the same size as the liquid particles something extraordinary takes place; the shavings develop a kind of 'useful schizophrenia', multiple identities. When portions of the ferrofluid are exposed to a magnetic field, the shavings remember their magnetic heritage and the fluid performs like a magnet; the rest of the time the shavings 'think' and act like a liquid. Like in appropriation of size and character of particles between the two substances here, significant lumping is dependent on an analysis of the systems at hand – with a bias towards finding latent correspondences – and fine-tuning these until they produce a desired but not entirely controlled effect. Lumpers are motivated by horizontal or lateral becoming, in which already complex identities merge into a single body and system: a systemic organic hybrid.'[1]

Derivation of the O/K Apartments

We would like, therefore, to introduce some issues in our work that we believe are connected to this notion of 'lumping', in particular, by using the Ost/Kuttner Apartments project as an example. The apartments were conceived as a network of 'sites', an active operational field of potential interventions. Upon identifying the sites, the design of cross-profiling was generated by using recombinative logic. Profiles of everyday domestic objects were cross-referenced according to their similarities and affinities. This was done in terms of morphology, performance, scale, programme, process-base and time (cross-categorical relationships). These relationships, characteristics and attributes were registered via computer software regardless of scale (cross-scalar

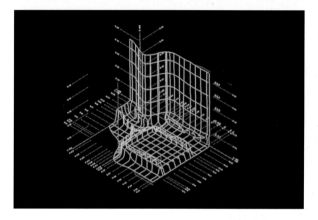

or 'appropriate' location. In turn, new formal and programmatic conditions were synthetically generated through multiply derived sets of these relationships and their nuances. These newly generated iterative derivations were unknown and impossible to preconceive or predict. This excess of (in) formation produces an interesting problem, inasmuch as it opens this field of synthetically generated material to intuition, interpretation and evaluation as architecture. Excess, in this instance, means ambiguity produced by a continually tuned set of rather precise relationships. The resulting topographies were conceived as 'ranges' that were always more or less of something else – more sleeping protocol, less bathing protocol or more storage protocol. The resulting domestic-scapes suggested an unfamiliar familiarity. This ambivalence towards form and programme as relational constructs provides for the possibilities of appropriating, adapting and adopting these structures for the particular needs and desires of the inhabitants.

In the case of the Ost/Kuttner Apartments, the composition of the inhabitants is constantly changing as they are 'corporate-private' and therefore used for family guests, visiting national and international business associates. The new topologies were invested with the body of the newly combined apartments. Unlike conventional separation by room, they do not register legible distinctions between space and programme.

Opposite
Detail of the aluminium-clad wardrobe/counter/stainless-steel sink/and medicine chest. A mirror is suspended over the counter. At the intersection of the aluminium wardrobe and glass wall is a 6-inch transparent panel that allows views of the most 'public' aspects of the private bath from Loft Space 1.

Right top
Three-dimensional construction isometric showing the multiple sections to be made into surfaces by cnc machines.

Right bottom
'Cross-profiling' concept diagram for the Ost/Kuttner Apartments; relationships of domestic products and items used in hybridising operations. The yields of these cross-profiling transformations are shown in scale and in location on site as domestic-scapes.

Above top
View of the kitchen/bath domestic-scape unit; door/ all surface sections are cut in plywood and aluminium and 'blocked' in foam.

Above bottom
View of the bed/bath domestic-scape unit; foamed, shaped and sanded to plywood forms.

Right
View of a fork-lift truck lifting the single-surface mould out of its forms after curing.

Above top
View of curing process at
the factory.

Above bottom
Overall view of the bed/bath
domestic-scape unit in the
factory.

Construction of the O/K Apartments
We were interested in continuing the project's
relationship to the computer from its derivation
(CAD) through to its manufacture (CAM). The site of
the project was a 'pre-World War II' (1933)
apartment building on the west side of Manhattan
between Central Park West and Columbus
Avenue. The building had only one original elevator
which was used for both passengers and services.
The apartment was not accessible by street or roof
crane for delivery of the computer-manufactured
(CAM) pieces. Since we were operating in very
difficult existing conditions it was necessary to

build stencils in the factory of the route from the lobby's
front door, via the elevator/hallways, to the pieces' final
positions in the apartments. To ensure trouble-free
delivery, a system of sectioning the 'scapes' for travel and
assembly on site was devised. This, also, affected the
sequencing of the construction of the apartments.

The 'fuselage' mould-building technique used high-
density fibreboard, plywood and aluminium slats cut with
computer numerically controlled (CNC) machines. (The
scaled vacuum-formed thermal plastic model was built
using a very similar mould technique.) This method can,
of course, quite easily be modified to produce unique
nonserial productions by simply replacing, rearranging or

81

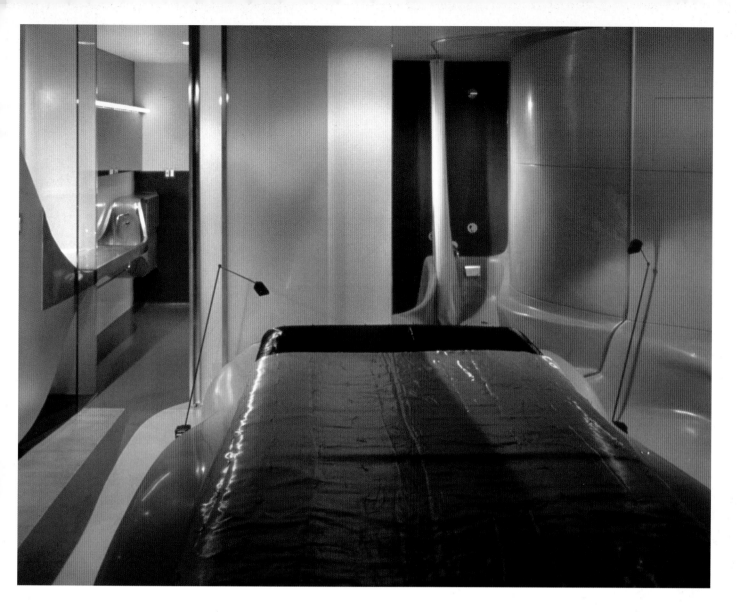

Opposite
Detail of bed/bath domestic-scape at the glass wall which forms the transparent limit of the bathing area. When full, the level of the water in the bath and sleeping surface of the bed align. Note the 'section of water' at glass wall.

Above
View of the orange fibreglass bed/bath domestic-scape with translucent sliding door and transparent glass wall system. The transparent wall allows for views of the more 'public' aspects of the private bath. In the foreground is the aluminium-clad wardrobe/counter/and stainless-steel sink. Also visible here are flat surfaces at the edge of the bed and at the ledge protrusion of the wall and bathtub. These areas are alternately used as dressing/make-up areas, reading alcove, seating area, storage shelf, etc.

Notes
1. Excerpt of a lecture and paper presented by Sulan Kolatan at 2000 Aspen Design Conference, Aspen, Colorado, USA.

reconfiguring these slats. (We are currently working on several larger projects which address this issue; some use variations of the 'fuselage' techniques described above.) As part of the process of building the mould, the interstitial spaces were filled with foam and shaved to the forms provided by the contours of the 'fuselage'. Then a hard coat was applied to receive the pigmented fibreglass layers. The removal of the moulds was facilitated by their smooth and curved morphologies. The fibreglass was chosen because it is a continuous (double-curving), self-supporting, durable and waterproof structure. The material was also chosen because it is 'a material without qualities'; meaning that fiberglass can mimic many textures ... or none in its suface. Engineering software was used to check its structure, and material stress and strain. These studies allowed the material to vary in thickness across its surface – the fibreglass was thickened where it needed strength, and thinner where it could be lighter.

Much of the strength of the pieces is gained through their curvature. They were moulded as single-surface pieces, based on the dimensional analysis of the site, then they were sectioned into three-dimensional 'jigsaw puzzle' parts that were

shiplapped on their exposed surfaces and typically bolted to each other on their hidden ones. On occasion both surfaces are exposed. If assembly is needed, it is done via a friction-slip joint fitted together with a modified detail of the shiplap connection. Fit was not an issue when working with these exacting tolerances.

Coordinated with the production of the fibreglass was the CNC cutting of the glass panels which needed to fit these irregular surfaces exactly. The fabric and upholstered constructions were made with a similar 'fuselage' technique. This meant that much of the responsibility for the dimensioning and method of construction had to be overseen by our office, in close collaboration with several manufacturers and subcontractors. The domestic-scapes were sequenced in the construction schedule so that the continuous self-levelling epoxy floor and wall system used their edges as forms to be poured against. Their bond forms a seamless edge, a liquid tectonic.

By using the example of the Ost/Kuttner Apartments, this discussion of 'lumping' is intended to demonstrate what we consider to be an operational 'feedback' between the formerly distinct categories of practice theory, design methods and construction techniques. ⚏

'Lumping' was first written by Sulan Kolatan and presented at the Aspen Design Conference, Colorado, in 2000.

Roller-Coaster
Construction

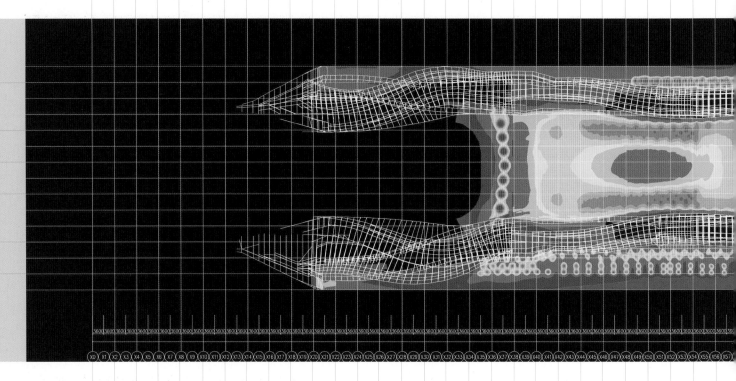

Foreign Office Architects demonstrate how to effectively exploit the potential offered by contemporary architectural techniques in order to initiate dynamic processes which produce new effects for contemporary conditions that are temporal and qualitative. **Alejandro Zaera-Polo** of FOA explains how they utilise the affective potential of architectural techniques to develop alternatives that master effects. For the Yokohama Port Terminal in Japan the office re-contextualised roller-coaster construction techniques in the building of these topological forms to produce new effects that resonate at different scales of spatial arrangement, structure and programme.

'This is where amateurs have an advantage over pros. A pro knows what he can deliver, and rarely goes beyond it. An amateur has no concept of his limitations and generally goes beyond them.' Trey Gunn, *Road Diaries*, Project Two Discipline Global Mobile 1998

Architecture is not a plastic art, but rather the construction of material life. Despite the classification, architecture is a plastic problem only if one decides upon plastic as the material; but that is just the particularity of architecture. This is what we hope serves to distinguish our work from other surface-complex architecture. We have grown tired of comparisons to Saarinen, Utzon or Gehry which, despite certain formal similarities and our appreciation of their work, are based purely on formal output. Formal resemblances are significant, but do not

existing etymologies. We are interested in exploring the processes of construction and engineering on a variety of levels, rather than creating structures that are the simple implementation of an idea, or merely the scaffolding of an image. A process generates the microhistory of a project, a kind of specific narrative where the entity of the project develops in a sequence. If geological, biological and human histories have something to teach us, it is that these processes of temporal formation produce organisations that possess far greater complexity and sophistication than instantaneous ideas. This is perhaps the most important contribution information technology has made to our practice: we can design, synthesise and proliferate specific histories and scripts for a project. Writing a project, as with Eisenman, involves the introduction of sequential development, rather than deployment of a former image. Proliferation entails waiting for the emergence of a project.

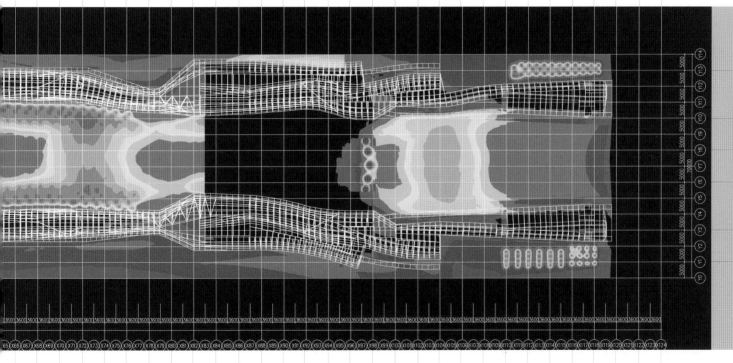

automatically imply similar approaches to process. For example, Gehry works in exactly the opposite direction to us, by producing a consistent spatial effect that is implemented through construction. Whereas our main priority is to produce consistency in the process that precedes construction and to avoid preconceived effects.

We want to 'unexplore' the materials; and here we should understand material in the broadest sense, as a source of ideas and effects. Processes are far less constraining than ideas, which are inherently linked to extant codes that operate critically, or in alignment, with pre-

We are no longer compelled to reproduce historical models, or to invent them from scratch. We do not have to design a project as the reproduction, derivation or invention of one. We do not need to bring about complexity by making collages: we can synthesise the processes of generation as an accelerated motion, adding information that becomes integral to the constructive process. This sequential, integrative addition produces effects that are increasingly more ambiguous, and more capable of resonating on different levels, than straightforward ideological statements, metaphors, allegories or reproductions.

Through our interest in the processes of construction and engineering of material life, we are led inevitably to

Above
Contour map: artificial lighting intensity.

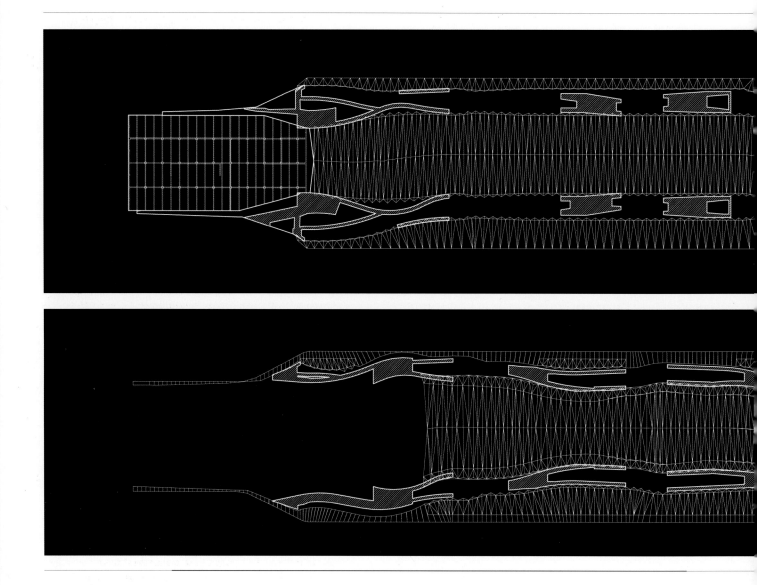

There is enormous potential yet to be discovered in the techniques of 'architectural services' that have not yet been exploited. For example, project management, estimation, surveys and the modelling capacity of artificial intelligence. None of these has yet been integrated into the discipline of architecture.

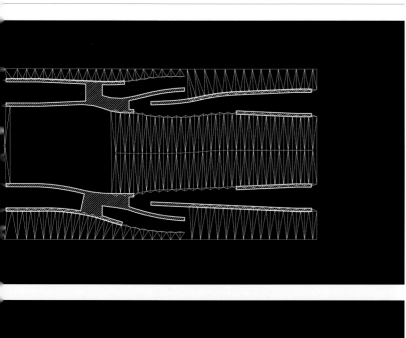

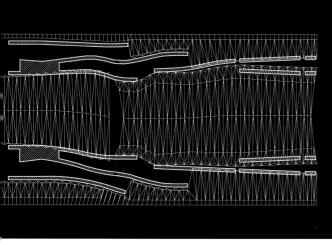

interface with varying technologies. Techniques are generally associated with performance, the production of effect and service delivery. Technique has become the domain of architectural services; but architecture as a service industry is a stifling business and rarely delivers compelling structures. The concept of architectural services derives from the interaction between architectural technology and effect. A skilled professional is capable of using specific techniques to produce specific effects. But what would happen if we were to divorce technique from service and effect? Is it possible to exploit the affective potential of architectural technique?

This is where one may find alternatives to architecture that master effects, at least those that are *a priori*. There is enormous potential yet to be discovered in the techniques of 'architectural services' that have not yet been exploited. For example, project management, estimation, surveys and the modelling capacity of artificial intelligence. None of these has yet been integrated into the discipline of architecture. This is leading the profession into an unhealthy and severe bifurcation between the performance of architectural luminaries and the banality of everyday service delivery. The real challenge is to utilise the potential of these technologies beyond their utilitarian association and to integrate them into a discipline that has remained static for too long.

A model for emulation is the ongoing fluidity of temporary and interdependent collaborations between musicians in the jazz community. One can observe the migration of techniques from Parker to Miles; and from Miles to Corea, Zawinul, Coltrane, etc. Of course, style must not be discarded: it is impossible to operate without it. But is it possible to generate it from technique? The fascination of jazz formations and lineage lies in witnessing how personal styles evolve in the process. There are areas of stylistic stability, and there are umbrellas that host drifters. Miles left behind umbrellas, as did Coleman, Coltrane and Zawinul after evolving through Mile's work and creating their own. And so it is with architectural umbrellas: the process of leaving them has nothing to do with marketing, management, time sheets, client portfolios and pension plans. It involves the production of knowledge, and requires a deep personal involvement from each participant.

In the creation of a project of this nature there is a precarious defence against the powerful forces that threaten continuously to stratify the work, and to return it to conventional processes. If one does not resist these forces, they may paralyse the project. These stifling obstacles include: greedy consultants; managers who measure the work according to time sheets and judge people by years of experience; mediocre client representatives who exhibit inherent mistrust of the

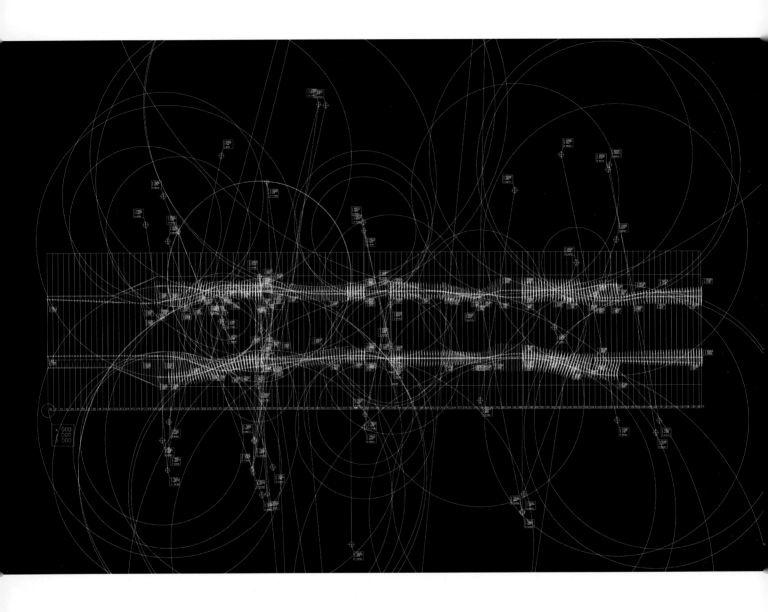

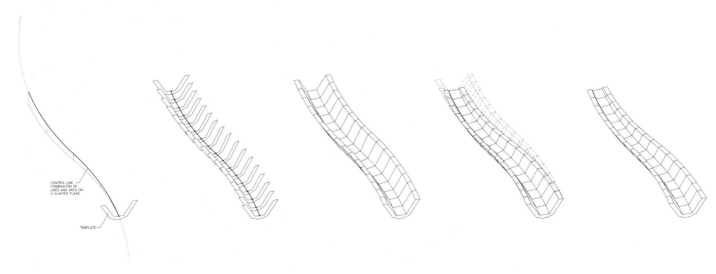

1. Defining a control line   2. Putting templates along the control line   3. Connecting templates with faces   4. Cutting out unnecessary parts   5. A piece of a ramp

young; obstructive engineers who cannot imagine anything beyond their calculator and ruler; and 'experienced' architects who no longer feel the need to learn, and who find it possible only to operate within a rigid hierarchical context.

Before embarking on a new project, it is essential that access to the latest technologies be provided, and that they play a central role in the production process. One must strive to remain centred within the research process, producing knowledge concomitant to the generation of the project in lieu of endeavouring merely to accumulate 'experience'. The structure that we proposed in the competition for the Yokohama Port Terminal comprised a folded piece of steel in an attempt to make the structure consistent with the general concept of the project as a folded organisation. This

enhancement for it to become realisable without betraying our purpose. The primary challenge was how to reconcile three-dimensional geometry with a geometry that, through folding, was essentially axial. Thus far, we have discovered unique geometric and formal emergences that have evolved from within the project itself, and have pre-empted external formal or geometric ideologies imposed from without. During the basic design phase, we devised a solution by which the folds of the web were interwoven at every half fold so that we could amplify the curvature. This is a structural geometry that has been used, for example, by Nervi, Piano and others to construct large-span shells with a structural unit or cell that is repeated along curves. Particularly of interest is the fact that the cells of the structure become differentiated at every point of the surface, much as in an organic system. One of the immediate results of this system was that we removed the lower plate of the structure to simplify the

Opposite top
Geometrical determination
of the girders/ramps.

Opposite bottom
Setting out of ramps.

Above left
Shinko side cantilevers.

Above middle
Girder end.

Above right
Girders.

proposal was also advantageous in terms of its resistance to earthquake stresses, and encompassed techniques of the naval industry to which the building was affiliated. The 'cardboard' structure emerged out of what originated as a reference to the local tradition of 'origami'. These references to local constructs, both literal and culturally mediated, were included for the purpose of contextualising the proposal while avoiding the mimicry of local structures. That is, the context was introduced as a process of material organisation, rather than as an image. This sensitivity to the locale played a decisive role in generating the building's geometry – for example, through the extraordinary importance placed on the latent asymmetry of the grounding conditions on site during the design phase.

In developing the design, structure was necessarily the critical focus of the project as our initial proposal needed substantial technical

construction. By making the folded metal plates a crucial expressive trait of the project, the origami was finally visible.

At this point, there was a debate over whether the structural system had to become an isotropic shell with local singularities, as the computer perspectives seemed to indicate, or whether it should retain the bidirectional qualities that the plan of the building contained. The latter would be a system composed of two series of large-scale folds, and bridged by a series of transversal folds. After testing what amounted to a hybrid of the original 'cardboard' type and a space frame with local densification, we realised that the concentration of axial stresses along the longitudinal large-scale folds would require alteration in order to become concrete-filled. This was the reason we decided that, despite the image of the building, the bidirectional structure was ultimately a more adequate solution. The coincidence between the ramp system and the main longitudinal girders became the primary determinant of the structural geometry, as the conflict between the symmetrical condition of the programmatic structure and the asymmetrical condition of the grounding system forced us to bend the ramps. The edges of the building were located 15 metres away from the pier's edges to comply with the symmetrical location of the boarding decks on both sides, while the foundations could only reach up to 21.5 metres from the Shinko side and 29 metres on the Yamashita side. This conflict between structural asymmetry and programmatic symmetry was already present in the competition entry, but had not been fully exploited due to absorption entirely in the lower level ramps, leaving the geometry of the upper level unaffected. It was only when we began to examine the correlation between the two levels of girders that the asymmetry was extended throughout the entire geometry. One of the

departure and arrival halls, and traffic plaza, which were linked locally through a deformed surface. That surface was constructed through a sequence of parallel transversal sections, referring to the local conditions every 15 metres, and morphing them along the axis of the building. The interesting question arising from the evolution of the grid was its location, ambiguously between an organisational technique based on parallel bands and the single-surface technique that absorbs differences into singularities of a congruent space. We were basically concerned with the single-surface effect, but our methods still relied on techniques learnt at OMA, where the sequences of parallel bands, developed from La Villette through the city hall in the Hague, and the Grand Bibliotheque, produced organisations that allowed for a maximum sectional flexibility. This could be thought of as a rotated 'plan libre', aimed at reaching maximum programmatic freedom across all levels. However, this meant that our programmatic aims –

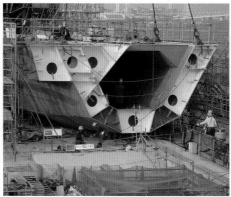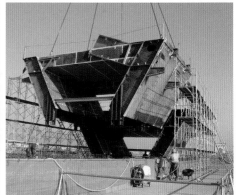

critiques we received after the competition scheme was made public contended that the topology of the building was basically symmetrical. While aware of this situation during the competition stage, we thought it more interesting to preserve the conflict as a generative trigger rather than imposing a formal ideology – symmetry – to the problem. Sensitivity to the initial conditions of the brief, and reference to the local shipbuilding industry were productive in the process of formal determination.

Another subject that has evolved throughout the development of the project has been the determination of the grid, the project's geometrical fabric. At the competition stage, analysing the spatial dynamics of the different functional areas throughout the terminal generated our proposal. The areas included the boarding decks, visitors' decks, roof-top plaza,

coherence of the circulation diagram across programs – were radically different from the programmatic incongruence of OMA's infamous band technique. The predominant longitudinal direction of the building and the essentially symmetrical programmatic structure supported the use of this organisation – hence producing a conflict with our interest in programmatic continuity that was supposed to drive the evolution of the project through detail design. The conflict between a striated organisation and a smooth congruence observed between the grounding conditions and the programmatic symmetry was also apparent in the juxtaposition of the project's aims and technique.

We would like to stress that despite its 'informal' appearance, our goal for this project – and most others – is a radical formal determination. The informal appearance is actually the direct result of highly complex and formally determinative processes. This is the aim of integrative addition as a method for organising the process. During the constant increase in the determination of the project's geometry, we began to enlarge the (1.5-metre) resolution of the transversal sections to a 5-metre resolution by inserting two new sections within each band. This technique was then used to determine the new intermediate sections by producing what we called 'control lines', or curves, determined by the location of each element in the transversal sections – boarding and visitors' decks, and parking halls. This was the first technique whereby we started to establish an argument of consistency between the different sections produced from the determinations within successive local conditions. By cutting the 'control lines' through intermediate planes, we were able to locate the position of the different elements longitudinally. At the same time, we transformed the splined geometry of the surface into a geometry of complex curves drawn from a

started the detailed design of the girder's geometry, it became apparent that even this amount of information was insufficient for precise control of the project. We also noticed that by rolling parallel sections along curved control lines we were producing irregularities in the geometry of the ramps unless we differentiated between the transversal sections of the girders. Even worse, because of the existing geometrical definition, all the girder faces would have to be triangulated, and different from each other, and every transversal fold would require a different geometry. Even if now we had control over the determination of the stiffeners that constructed the girders, we still had no control over the triangulation of their faces. One of the most important evolutions in the project occurred at this point. We started to consider the construction of the girders through the rotation of the same stiffener templates at regular intervals along the 'control lines' that also now had to be dropped into complex curves. In order to

palette of seven radiuses. The resulting surface was produced from the intersection of cylindrical, or conical, surfaces of regular radiuses in order to simplify the manufacturing procedure. This process produced 96 transversal sections which determined the building's form, but lacked sufficient detail for the actualisation of the project. Due to a change in the basic size of the transversal folds, we increased the resolution to a grid of 3.6 metres, while still using the 'control curves' as our method of coherence. Subsequently, the 124 transversal sections were doubled as the basic scale of the transversal folds was fixed at 1.8 metres, which became the new resolution of the grid.

The process of geometrical development basically involved increasing the resolution of the grid, and every step in this process required an exponential increase in the amount of information required for production. When we

increase the regularity of the manufacturing process, we began to consider the possibility of producing local symmetry in the transversal folds, by making them meet the girders at a perpendicular angle. The only way to achieve this, given the deformed geometry of the girders, was to shift from the parallel transversal grid of the competition entry to a topological grid originating in the control lines that determined the girders' geometry. In our new topological grid, the parallel bands did not grant independence to the different parts. On the contrary, they established functions that connected them to each other, considerably diminishing the amount of information required for the determination of the form. We had therefore moved from a 'raster' space, where each point is determined by local information, to a vectorial space, where each point is determined by differentiated global orders. Again, there was no ideological or critical statement implied by taking this step; it was simply the pragmatic resolution of technical conflicts in the process of development. These types of discoveries can turn processes of a purely technical nature into architectural discipline. They allow the discipline to emerge from the production rather than from a critical or ideological relation to the previous constitution of the discipline.

The next conflict that emerged was in the choice between repetition in the girder's geometry and symmetry in the transversal folds. Since the folds would have to link with the girders at the stiffeners' locations, if we wanted localised symmetry of the folds we would have to sacrifice regularity in the girders' sections. Hence the pitch of the stiffeners would be determined by the intersection of the folds with the girder's edge. If, conversely, we started with a regular pitch of the stiffeners in the girders, we would have to

steel weight was concentrated in the girders, we decided to make a grid that was determined by rolling templates along the 'control lines' at regular intervals, so that the girders' construction would become as regular as possible. With this decision, the fabric of the folds had to become antimetrical in the central folds – still identical in terms of formal determination – and symmetrical on the lateral folds, leaving only the two intermediate folds of every arch to be irregular. A third scale of folding was produced at this stage and, to reduce the total weight of steel, we had to place small stiffeners inside the small-scale transversal folds. This would cause substantial increases in the manufacturing costs. In order to avoid this, we decided to replace the 6-millimetre-thick plates that constituted the first proposal for the detail of the folds with a 3.2-millimetre corrugated plate. The corrugations provide the plates with enough strength to avoid the stiffeners. The process is not yet finished, although most of the crucial

sacrifice the local symmetry of the folds. In order to set up a nonparallel grid for solving the problem, we gave priority to the local symmetry of the folds for determining the position of the stiffeners along the girders. The position of the new grid lines was not geometrically determined, and had to be calculated numerically through a program that established iteration loops to calculate the intersection of the transversal folds' local axis with the curved edges of the girders.

As a program, the iteration loops had to be calculated sequentially so that the results would depend on the area of the plan where we began calculating them. However, due to the fact that after calculation over 65 per cent of

decisions have already been made. In one recent meeting with the contractors they asked us for the coordinates of the points of the building, as if the form had already been decided, *a priori,* and they needed only to implement that geometry on site. They were shocked when we explained to them that the geometry was strictly related to the manufacturing and construction systems, and could be modified if necessary. They were under the impression that site control was to be the most crucial aspect of the construction process. One of them pointed out that the same technique is used to build roller-coasters, where the setting out utilises local references between identical templates rolled along irregular three-dimensional geometry. 'Exactly!' we said, 'Roller-coaster construction!' ◬

Above left
Ramp connection from terminal to roof plaza.

Above middle
Terminal level ceiling.

Above right
View of terminal level under construction.

Virtually Crash Testing the Box

Jeff Turko explores the potential of transferring crash-testing techniques common to the automotive industry to architecture. He stresses the need to address effects, environment and emergent conditions in ways similar to the automotive industry to create 'an instrumental trajectory for the discipline' capable of producing highly performative effects that can validate the effectiveness of their generative techniques. This article reveals the potential for new techniques that will become viable for architecture in the not so distant future.

Though architecture's greatest achievements have occurred as artistic effects, as pleasure of eye and mind, its deepest desire is to ply its techniques as a life shaping force.
Jeffrey Kipnis

In the automotive industry the notion of crash testing products, virtually and actually, in as many possible conditions they can be set in is imperative. Of course, this is done for the success of business, and for the safety and happiness of customers. But the interesting outcome of the techniques is that they pinpoint both predictable and unpredictable effects. The exposure of these effects, and using the techniques to set up the conditions that generated them, points towards new types of solutions and conditions that have not yet been revealed. It is this outcome of 'effect' that highlights these virtual techniques, and reveals the potential for applying them to architecture and other design disciplines. When one looks more closely at the techniques employed in virtual crash testing it is evident that this is a wide-ranging and complex world to sift through.

It is not just about simulating the impact of a rapidly moving car into a solid object – it involves the total environment. For example, the directionality in which the body panels deform when impacted, or when impacting another car, how much the passenger environment deforms on impact, what internal injuries might be sustained by the passenger.

The automotive industry has been in operation for about a century. Compared with the evolutionary processes of architecture, it has developed at a much more rapid pace, with virtual simulation playing an integral part in the manufacturing process. With the demand for rapid and cost-effective design cycles, virtual simulations have become a competitive necessity for car manufacturers. The variables of an unforeseen collision, or what could be termed an emergent condition, have also driven the development of multitudinal techniques. The unpredictable complexity of the driving environment is so vast that the quickest and most cost-effective way to remain abreast of current road conditions is to run simulations and test all possibilities.

Virtual crash testing (VCT) is specific of necessity. Within it, the construct of the environment must be

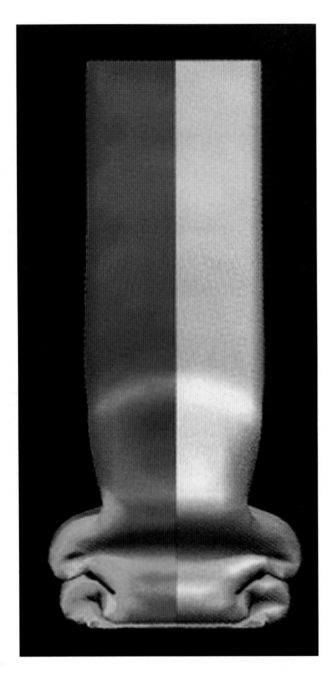

amounts of fallen leaves from neighbouring trees that are filtered along the driver's path? How many people are simulated in the car: one, two or an entire family? Are they men or women and approximately what age? Specific parametric input is vital to VCT. The accuracy of the set-up is what validates the effects that are generated. Only then is the operation useful to the design process.

Technically the setting up is done through software such as PAM-CRASH, a physics-based program that is written to run on Windows NT or Unix platforms and developed by ESIGroup, a company that has been working with nonlinear mechanics since 1973. A program like this comes with many different parametric constraints already in place such as common materials associated with engineering – metals, plastics and composites. One can then model extreme nonlinear material behaviour under high loads, testing the elastic and plastic behaviour of materials under different strain rates. This is simply one example of what a program like this is capable of achieving. Companies such as the ESI Group are leaders in the development of these types of simulation technologies, which take into account all the events and techniques that can occur in the process of building the car. Their technology is used to test everything from oil-tanker collisions to aerodynamic forces, electromagnetic interference, stress analysis, welding and heat treatment, high-velocity impacts and passenger safety to name just a few. They have even extended their knowledge to develop other areas of the automotive manufacturing process. ESI Group and similar companies have shown the value of acknowledging effects as a prime aspect of design through the development of their technology and techniques.

So how does one start to crash test a building? As architects, we create environments that are not quite as unpredictable as that of a motorway but which do contain their own set of complex variables. Effects, environment and emergent conditions are issues we would do well to address in ways similar to those of the automotive industry. At present, I would argue, we do not attribute to them the significance they deserve. These issues should be shifted to the front of the discourse and the profession. Imagine testing all the built environments and possible conditions of use that may take shape within our buildings and spaces? What will the results tell us about our formal, strategic and material moves? Hopefully, they will start to inform us of the effects we have, and can achieve, in our environments through our formal, strategic and material moves. If architecture can test and perpetuate itself based on the effects it produces, we may be able to brush off the baggage of its past, and create for the discipline an instrumental trajectory towards highly performative environments. ⌂

made as close to reality as possible. The simulated vehicle needs to be as accurate as one that is to be driven off a showroom floor. The different types of material make-up of the car must be exact and must factor in subtleties from the inner mechanics of the engine to the variability of the drivers' environment. Even the specifics of the context must be calculated accurately. Is the wall that is being hit just a wall of bricks? Or is it a reinforced concrete wall that has a thickness of 500 millimetres with a brick facing? How has the driving surface been constructed? For example, has the surface been wet for approximately 10 minutes, with a ground temperature of 2° Celsius and generous

Biographies/Credits

Cecil Balmond is the chairman of the Europe and Building board and a main board member of Ove Arup. Having initially studied engineering and carried out research in pure mathematics and chemistry, he is now best known for his collaborations with experimental architects, such as Rem Koolhaas, Daniel Libeskind, Enrique Miralles and van Berkel that have spanned more than 30 years. He teaches at Harvard and Yale, and is the author of *Number 9* (1999) and *Informal*, to be published in March 2002.

Johan Bettum is the leader of the PCMA research programme at the Oslo School of Architecture, Norway, 2000–2002. For more information on its collaborators and sponsors, as well as its objectives see www.ifid.aho.no/pcma/about/aho.html. Bettum lectures and teaches internationally. He has taught at the AA in London and UCLA in the US and is currently Guest Professor at the Städeoschule in Frankfurt, Germany. Bettum is also a partner in the newly started architecural studio, Tupelo Architecture, and a former member of the architecture and design group OCEAN in Oslo.

Project credits for Holiday Inn Express Hotel, Sandefjord International Airport, Norway, 1998–2001. PCMA team: Johan Bettum, Steinar Killi (rapid prototype model and finite element analyses), Lina Aker, Heidi Ekstrøm Devik, Randi-Lise Almas, Magnus Petterson and Dan Sevaldson. Catia sponsorship: IBM Norway. Preliminary design OCEAN north team: OCEAN Oslo Johan Bettum, Bonsak Schieldrop, Kim Baumann-Larsen and Birger Sevaldson; OCEAN Cologne Michael Hensel; OCEAN Helsinki Kivi Sotamaa and Lasse Wager. Collaborators: Ludo Grooteman, Blue Architecture and Urbanism (Amsterdam), Kjell Dybedal, Kalvert & Clarke (Oslo). Project members: Ville Martin and Corey Rubadue.

Bernard Cache is the leading principal of the Paris-based design and software company Objectile, which he founded in 1996 with Patrick Beaucé and Jean-Louis Jammot. He has taken an important role as a senior consultant in major strategic studies on image telecommunications and digital television for companies such as Philips, Canal Plus and France Telecom. He has written widely on communication policy and economics as well as architecture. He has most recently held academic appointments as Associate Professor of Architectural Design and Computing at the University of Toronto, Visiting Professor at the Universidad Internacional de Catalunya and Visiting Professor at the School of Architecture, UCLA.

Manuel DeLanda is the author of three major philosophical books, *War in the Age of Intelligent Machines* (1991), *A Thousand Years of Nonlinear History* (1997) and *Intensive Science and Virtual Philosophy* (2002). He teaches two seminars at the School of Architecture, Columbia University: 'Philosophy of History: Theories of Self-Organization and Urban Dynamics'; and 'Philosophy of Science: Thinking about Structures and Materials'.

Kolatan/MacDonald Studio. Sulan Kolatan and William MacDonald are partners in Kolatan/MacDonald Studio, which they founded in 1988, in New York City. Both principals teach at Columbia University's Graduate School of Architecture, Planning

and Preservation. In addition to receiving numerous awards, such as the 48th Annual Progressive Architecture Award and 44th Annual Progressive Architecture Citation, 1999 AIA Projects Award and the Forty under Forty Award, the work produced by Kolatan/ MacDonald Studio is in the permanent collections of the Museum of Modern Art in New York, the Deutsches Architektur Museum in Frankfurt, the FRAC in Orleans, the San Francisco Museum of Modern Art and the Avery Library Collection. Currently, their office is working on a residential compound for Ms. Ost and Mr. Kuttner in Virginia (the clients of the O/K Apartments).

Project Credits for Ost/Kuttner Apartments. Principals in charge: Sulan Kolatan and William J MacDonald. Team: E Schoenenberger, N Cunningham, S Doub, M Hollis, R Carpenter, P Palmgren, P Walsch. Clients: Beatrix Ost and Ludwig Kuttner. Engineers: Guy Nordenson and Leo Argiris, Partners; Ove Arup Associates. Contractors: E Wong and S Sumaida of Foundations Design International, Inc; Seal Reinforced Concrete Inc; J Depp Glass, Inc. Model: J Masibay of Breadbox Studio.

Michael Hensel and **Kivi Sotamaa** are partners in the Helsinki-based design office OCEAN north together with Tuuli Sotamaa and Birger Sevaldson. Michael Hensel teaches in the Emergent Technologies and Design Programme at the Architectural Association in London. Kivi Sotamaa is a research fellow at the University of Art and Design in Helsinki.For more information see www.ocean-north.net.

Project Credits for a_drift NYT Time (finalist in invited design competition by the *New York Times*, 1999). OCEAN north team: Kivi Sotamaa (project coordination), Tuuli Sotamaa, Birger Sevaldson, Michael Hensel, Johan Bettum. Consultant: Tero Kolhinen, Institute of Metallurgie, University of Helsinki.

Project credits for Intencities (Installation Project for ArtGneda 2000, as part of Helsinki Cultural Capital 2000) Production: Kaisa Kivelä; Architecture OCEANNORTH Kivi Sotamaa (project coordination), Michael Hensel, Tuuli Sotamaa; Project Members: Lasse Wager, Stephane Valcroze, Toni Kauppila; Dance: GRUPPEN FYRA Vera Nevanlinna, Pia Tavela, Jenni Laitnen, Sanna Koskela; Costumes; Maria Duncer; Fine Arts: Janne Räisänen; Graphic Design: Klaus Haapaniemi; New Media: KATASTRO.Fl Mika Huthamäki, Juha Huuskonen, Jani Isoranta, Mikko Karvonen, Mikko Wilkman; New Media: Juha Fiilin.

Greg Lynn has taught throughout the United States and Europe and is presently Professor of Spatial Conception and Exploration at the ETH in Zurich, a studio professor at UCLA (where parts of the Predator was manufactured) and the Davenport Visiting Professor at Yale University. His office, Greg Lynn FORM, is presently designing a 500 unit housing block transformation of the Kleiburg Block in the Bijlmermeer outside of Amsterdam, the Uniserve Corporate Headquarters in Los Angeles along with a variety of design projects including a coffee and tea service for Alessi, a book container for *Visionaire* Magazine and a series of large scale architectural lighting and furniture elements for Max Protetch Gallery in New York City. He is the author of *Animate Form* (Princeton Architectural Press), *Folds, Bodies and Blobs: Collected Essays* (La letter volee) and the forthcoming *Embryological House*. His work has been exhibited internationally in both architecture and art museums and galleries.

The artist **Fabian Marcaccio** collaborated with Greg Lynn on the 'Predator' exhibition at the Wexner Center for the Arts in Columbus,

Ohio (27 January – 15 April 2001). Currently living and working in New York, Marcaccio was born in Argentina in 1963 where he attended the University of Philosophy, Rosario de Santa Fe. During 2002, he is exhibiting at the Gallerie Thaddeus Ropac Gallery, Salzburg, Austria; Joan Prats Gallery, Barcelona, Spain; Gorney Bravin + Lee, New York; and Kevin Bruk Gallery, Miami, Florida (with Teresita Fernandez).

Ali Rahim guest-edited the highly successful *Contemporary Processes in Architecture*, *Architectural Design*, vol 70, no 3, 2000. He is the principal of Contemporary Architecture Practice in New York City and currently teaches at the University of Pennsylvania.

Project Credits for Introduction, Contemporary Techniques in Architecture. Design research: Ali Rahim (principal), John Cooney, Brian Kimura and Lee Rubenstein (design assistants); Nathaniel Hadley, Yuchuan Chang (assistants).

Project Credits for 'Potential Performative Effects'. Research assistant: Anne Kojima. Design research: Ali Rahim (principal), Yuchuan Chan, Nathaniel Hadley, Beatrice Witzgall (design assistants); Marci Songcharoen, Michel Hsiung (assistants).

Preston Scott Cohen is an Associate Professor at Harvard Design School. He is author of *Contested Symmetries and Other Predicaments in Architecture* (Princeton Architectural Press, 2001). Recent projects include short-list design proposals for the temporary Museum of Modern Art, and the Museum of Art and Technology, both in New York. Recent exhibitions include 'Folds, Blobs and Boxes' at the Carnegie Museum of Art (2001), 'Archilab 2001' in Orleans, 'The Un-Private House' at the Museum of Modern Art in New York (1999) and 'Home' in Glasgow (1999). He is represented by the Thomas Erben Gallery in New York.

Project credits for the Museum of Art and Technology. Eyebeam Atelier project team: Preston Scott Cohen (design): Cameron Wu, Chris Hoxie; CR Studio Architects (associate architects) Lea Cloud, Victoria Rospond, principals: Jon Dreyfous, Chris Hoxie, Jay Stancil, Sally Zambrano-Olmo, Kristin Enderlein, Adrienne Broadbear, Feliz Skamser. Visualisation: Chris Hoxie, Cameron Wu. Animation, production design: K+D Lab, Dean D Simone, Joseph Kozinski (principals), Brandon Hicks. Virtual installation pieces by metaphrenie.com. Video production: Robert Michaels. Consultants: Robert Heintges (curtain wall), Guy Nordenson (structural), Karen Sideman (curatorial).

Servo is David Erdman-Los Angeles, Marcelyn Gow-Zurich, Switzerland, Ulrika Karlsson- Stockholm, Sweden and Chris Perry-New York City. David Erdman teaches studios and seminars at UCLA, Los Angeles and RPI, Marcelyn Gow at the ETH, Zurich, Ulrika Karlsson at the KTH, Stockholm and Chris Perry at Pratt, Coumbia College and RPI. Servo was one of six design collaboratives which participated in the 2001 Young Architects Forum at the Architectural League of New York and are currently artists in residence at the IASPIS Foundation in Stockholm, Sweden. They are currently working on projects for exhibitions at the Wexner Center for the Arts and The Cooper Hewitt Smithsonian National Design Museum.

Project credits for 'Servoline' and 'Nurbrest': Servo. Project Design Assistants: Jonas Runberger, Daniell Norell, Nina Lorber, Ulrika Wachmeister, Alice Deitsch, Johan Bohlin, Oskar Jonsson, John Stack. Consultants: Cult 3D, Prototal AG.

Project credits for 'Cloudline': Servo. Project Design Assistants:

Emily Grandstaff, Jay Hindmarsh, Jung Oh. Consultants: Cambridge Valley Machining, RPI Advanced Manufacturing Lab

Project credits for'Cloudcurtain' Project Design: Servo. Project Design Assistants: Jeremy Schacht. Consultants: University of California, LA

Kristina Shea is a lecturer in engineering design at Cambridge University (UK) and a co-director of the Engineering Design Centre. Current support is provided by a Philip Leverhulme prize through the Leverhulme Trust (UK). The technique presented originated as a PhD thesis advised by Jon Cagan at Carnegie Mellon University (USA) and was funded by the NSF (USA).

Project credits for 'Creating Synthesis Partners'. Renderings and collaboration for conceptualisation of the marina: Janet Fan (MIT) and Larry Sass (MIT).

Peter Testa and **Devyn Weiser** founded and direct the Emergent Design Group at MIT with Una-May O'Reilly of the MIT Artificial Intelligence Lab. Testa and Weiser are involved in creative partnerships with a number of industries developing new building systems. Their work is widely published and exhibited internationally, most recently at SIGGRAPH '99 and '01. Testa is also Associated Architect with Álvaro Siza on several current projects including the Art Center College of Design in Pasadena.

Project credits for 'Emergent Structural Morphology'. Emergent Design Group, MIT: Peter Testa, Una-May O'Reilly, Devyn Weiser with Markus Kangas, Axel Kilian, Simon Greenwold, Martin Hemberg, Ben Piper, Janet Fan. http://mit.edu/edgsrc

Jeffrey Turko is a principal member of Urban-Office and a collaborator in OCEAN north. He has taught at the Architectural Association and is currently teaching at the University of East London. He is also a founding member of the do-group (www.do-group.net), a noncommercial, international transdisciplinary think-tank that conducts experimental research and design. www.urban-office.com; email: jeffturko@urban-office.net

Michael Weinstock is currently Master of Technical Studies at the Architectural Association in London, and his personal research includes urbanism, ballet (in collaboration with the choreographer Gaby Agis) and the convergence of emergent technologies and architecture.

Alejandro Zaera-Polo and **Farshid Moussavi** are directors of Foreign Office Architects Limited. The practice was founded in 1996 in London when the principals won the competition for the Yokohama International Port Terminal in Japan, which is to be completed in March 2002. As well as their work on Yokohama, they are currently constructing projects in London, Spain and South Korea. They have been widely exhibited and published internationally, and were short-listed in 2001, along with Raphael Viñoly, for their designs for the South Bank Centre in London. www.f-o-a.net

Project credits for Yokohama International Port Terminal (detail design and supervision phase): Farshid Moussavi, Alejandro Zaera-Polo with Kensuke Kishikawa, Yasuhisa Kikuchi, Izumi Kobayashi, Kenichi Matsuzawa, Tomofomi Nagayama, Xavier Ortiz, Lluís Viú Rebes and Keisuke Tamura. Local architect consultant: GKK Architects, Japan. Structural engineers: Structural Design Group, Japan. Mechanical and electrical engineers: PT Morimura. Competition design team: Farshid Moussavi, Alejandro Zaera-Polo with Iván Ascanio, Yoon King Chong, Michael Cosmas, Jung-Hyun Hwang, Guy Westbrook. Competition engineering advisors: Ove Arup & Partners. First executive design phase, design team: Farshid Moussavi, Alejandro Zaera-Polo with Félix Bendito, Jordi Mansilla, Kenichi Matsuzawa and Santiago Triginer. Second executive design phase, design team: Farshid Moussavi, Alejandro Zaera-Polo with Victoria Castillejos, Dafne Gil, Kenichi Matsuzawa, Oriol Monfort, Xavier Ortiz, Lluís Viú Rebes, José Saenz, Julián Varas and Thomasine Wolfensberger.

98+ Interior Eye:
Archi-Tectonics, Aida Hair Salon
Craig Kellogg

102+ Engineering Exegesis:
Lightweight Structures
Bas Veldman and Oscar Mölder

108+ **Beat the Devil**
Diane Lewis

113+ Building Profile
Climate Prediction Center
Jeremy Melvin

118+ Practice Profile:
S333
Lucy Bullivant

124+ **Highlights from Wiley-Academy**

125+ **Book Reviews**

126+ **Site Lines**

Archi-Tectonics,
Aida Hair Salon

In fair weather, direct southern sunlight projects the salon name from where it is sandblasted near the bottom of the storefront window. The shadow tattoos the floor at the waiting area. Winka Dubbeldam is responsible for all built-in components, as well as the logo and architectural signage.

Interior Eye

In this new Δ+ series that specialises in interior space, regular contributor Craig Kellogg looks at a hairdressing salon on the Upper East Side of New York whose internal architecture takes its cue from the hard plastic shells of high-performance cycling crash helmets.

It's to the great credit of architect Winka Dubbeldam that we have anything at all to say in this magazine about the design of a hair salon. The essential elements – mirror, counter, chair – are usually considered furniture, not architecture. And the assembly-line flow of a salon, where hair is cleaned at a wet station then cut or styled elsewhere, is neither a complicated nor a very interesting spatial puzzle to solve. As Dubbeldam notes, 'The most important thing is to create an interesting problem.' Asked to redesign an ordinary 2000-square-foot storefront for its new tenant, the Aida salon, Dubbeldam took her inspiration, eventually, from a close inspection of high-performance cycling crash helmets. Just under the hard plastic shell is an elegant passive ventilation system. The thick rigid foam padding is tunnelled with channels that deliver to the scalp the air streaming past a moving rider. Taken together, the foam and the shell are what Dubbeldam terms a 'smart skin'.

So the Aida salon would have a hard, white skin to wrap its services – a smart shell embedded with lighting, audio, ventilation and power points. Dubbeldam projected systems for the salon against the sides of the boxy existing interior. Then she specified a faceted 'wrapper' of flat gypsum board panels on steel studs to cover them. Clearly, right angles hold no particular fascination for her. The construction contractor joined Dubbeldam's tessellated panels simply, with the minimum fanfare. Crisp creases mark the joints of broad neighbouring facets.

As an early proponent of computer-aided design, Dubbeldam designs primarily with three-dimensional digital models. (Before integrated CAD technology existed, she would translate section cuts from her virtual volumes into hand-drawn construction documents.) Nevertheless, the Aida salon barely resembles work by other digital architects. This may stem, in part, from the fact that the scheme was driven largely by practical concerns. The walls at Aida are 'informed constantly by what they do', she explains. Conveniently, where a shelf is needed at the cutting stations, the vertical surface of the skin folds into a counter. Vanity lighting at the mirrors is slotted into the thickness of the wall so fluorescent sources are not visible. Stripping the space to its geometry is a way 'architecture can become an environment. I'm not necessarily interested in objects,' Dubbeldam explains.

Although her clients would be young and fashionable, building an interior landscape of seamless subtlety wasn't necessarily an obvious choice for owner Aida Alvarado, who lives and works on the Upper East Side of Manhattan. Though

bare fluorescent tubes glare down on plenty of nearby dry-cleaning and grocery shops, the neighbourhood is also known for retailers who ape the tired, olde-worlde look of the French countryside. Fortunately Dubbeldam, for her part, would not dream of participating in that charade. 'I come from Europe – we want to move forward,' she says. 'It insults the past to imitate it.' Walking the fine line between theme and theatre, she has opted for timelessness, pure geometry and 'very soft modulations'. In a place where stylists' clients have 'little to do but observe', delicately folded planes, light, and shadow supply fascinating but abstract entertainment. ⌀

As architect of Manhattan's Aida salon, Winka Dubbeldam knew well the kind of feeling the client needed for her new location. The architect, who was profiled in American *Vogue* in September 2001, is herself part of the salon's stylish target market. Though a foreigner (born in Holland), Dubbeldam has worked in the New York offices of both Bernard Tschumi and Peter Eisenman. She graduated from Rotterdam's Institute of Higher Education, Faculty of Arts and Architecture, then in 1992 received a master's degree from Columbia University. She has worked for BOA architects Rotterdam and Steven Holl Architects. Currently, she is an adjunct assistant professor of architecture at Columbia University, and the University of Pennsylvania in Philadelphia. Since founding the New York firm Archi-Tectonics, in 1994, her commissions have included a freestanding suburban house now under construction, apartments, loft renovations and offices. 'I started with a small art gallery. I did an urban design for Moscow,' she notes, adding, 'I'm happy doing a hair salon.'

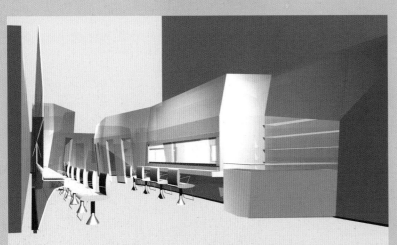

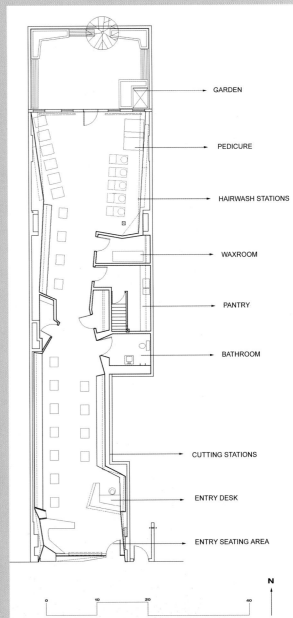

GARDEN

PEDICURE

HAIRWASH STATIONS

WAXROOM

PANTRY

BATHROOM

CUTTING STATIONS

ENTRY DESK

ENTRY SEATING AREA

N

0   10   20   40

Below
Study of Aida Hair Salon. In order from top:
programme analysis, surface inflection, total insertion.

Below bottom left and right
Perspective and total insertion of 'smart wall' system.

Below top
Floor plan of 2000-square-foot salon.

Below middle
Framing the storefront are mitered slabs of bluestone, a tough natural
material used for New York City sidewalks. Hollow gypsum board interior
walls continue the language of planes that originates outside the glass.

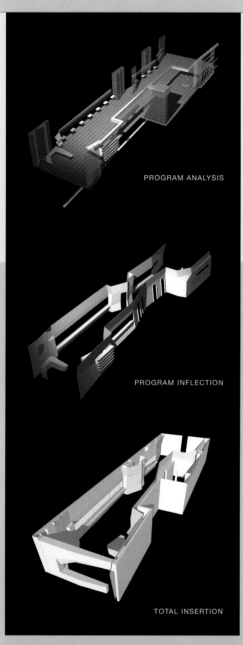

PROGRAM ANALYSIS

PROGRAM INFLECTION

TOTAL INSERTION

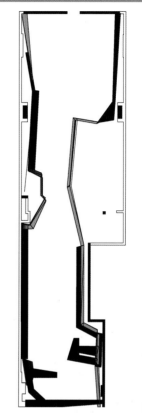

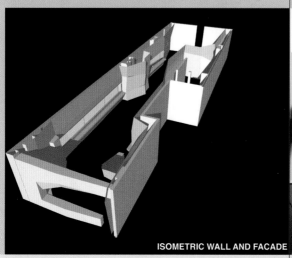

ISOMETRIC WALL AND FACADE

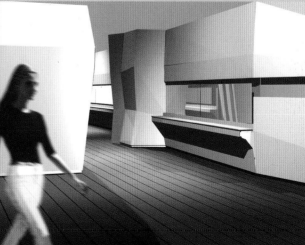

Lightweight Structures

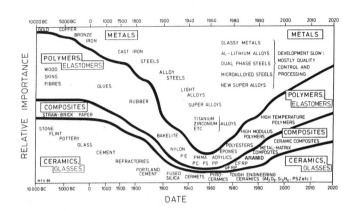

Above left
Ashby's curve

The evolution and the change in relative importance of construction materials over history is remarkable. The graph in the shape of a not very comfortable bathtub, as drawn by Ashby, roughly shows what happened in the past and what is bound to happen in the future. Ten thousand years ago, the nomadic people had to rely on lightweight materials, which can be seen as the predecessors of today's advanced composite materials, mixtures of straw and mud and tent structures. As time went by, people settled themselves, and started to use other materials such as brick, and metals for weaponry. In the 20th century the use of metals reached its climax. From the 1960s, the use of advanced composite materials saw a rapid increase to meet the demand to lower structural weight.

Above right and right
Black tent

The 'black tent' is a typical example of a lightweight nomadic habitat. The tent is constructed out of a fabric made of hair from goats, sheep, camels or yaks. This fabric is supported by tent poles and tension wires. The black colour of the tent is remarkable since it absorbs heat. One would think this an unfavorable colour but on the contrary. The dark cloth is a fine example of combining functions in a light and strong material. The cloth provides shade and absorbs heat because the loose weave allows the heat to disperse. Hair is also able to provide insulation against cold. Tents can be seen over a wide range of climates, the black tent in deserts and the circular white tent or Yurt in the icy planes of Mongolia.

This article is the first in a new series of engineering articles conceived for Δ+ with the aid of a specially appointed think tank. The panel includes Adriaan Beukers from the aerospace department of the University of Technology in Delft, Max Fordham of Max Fordham & Partners, Tony Hunt of Anthony Hunt and Associates and André Chaszar of Buro Happold in New York. The aim of the series is to effectively communicate to architects cutting-edge engineering ideas and innovations. The initial topic for discussion is that of 'lightness', as so potently advocated in Adriaan Beuker and Ed van Hinte's book of the same title. Here Bas Veldman and Oscar Mölder from the aerospace department of the University of Technology in Delft look at how lightness might best be achieved through various types of lightweight structures.

Lightweight Fabric Structures: A Renaissance

Lightness, Adriaan Beuker and Ed van Hinte's highly accessible manifesto arguing for minimum energy structures, has had a revelatory impact on the way we view weight in architecture. On its publication in 1997, it brought to international attention the perhaps obvious but largely ignored fact that, simply by striving to construct vehicles and built structures that are lighter, energy consumption can fundamentally be reduced. These are not new lessons to be learnt. Beukers and van Hinte describe their stance as that of a 'renaissance' (the book is subtitled 'The inevitable renaissance of minimum energy structures'). The basic premise of their argument is that we have a lot to learn from the artefacts of ancient nomadic cultures which carried all their possessions with them. Objects such as tents, chariots and bows are all finely balanced composite constructions that evolved over thousands of years. The main theme of the book is thus synergy of different materials. A synergy that can be reasserted today with the use of smart combinations of fibres and plastics, and through an awareness of how critical the balance of the 'trinity' of material, shape and the process of making is in the creation of lighter constructions.

Fabric structures were invented long ago because when people first left tropical Africa to conquer the rest of the world it was necessary to carry the environment of the tropics with them. Therefore they needed cloth, first skins and later man-made fibre fabrics, which kept the tropical warmth next to the skin – a portable climate. Nomadic people also needed to develop lightweight habitats or tent structures. These used a combination of tension and compression members and can be seen as predecessors of tensegrity structures. Two constructive principles for tent structures evolved.[1] One uses tent poles and tension wires to span a fabric, the other uses a self-supporting wooden framework draped with mats.

The use of materials is always accompanied by constructive concepts, in a symbiotic relationship. Ashby describes a trend towards the increased use of composite materials in the future.[2] Combined with this, is the development of the engineering discipline of designing tensegrity structures. Nowadays, a designer has advanced nonlinear FEM (Finite Element Method) computer programs at his disposal to efficiently design lightweight fabric structures.

In the 20th century a new type of lightweight fabric structure was erected: the inflatable building. Such structures are based on a pressure differential over a membrane that creates tensile stresses that result in the structure being able to bear compression loads. The structure is only able to cope with compressive loads for as long as the membrane stress is tensile. Comprehensive stresses cannot exist in a thin membrane so wrinkles occur once the membrane stress becomes zero. Inflatable buildings can be divided into two categories: air-supported structures and air-inflated structures.

Air-supported Structures

The earliest attempt to use an air-supported structure in architecture was Lanchester's proposal for an air-supported hall in 1917.[3] He did not see any of his air-supported designs realised, partly because suitable materials and manufacturing techniques were not available, but mainly because this type of construction was not yet acceptable to the public. Other designers copied Lanchester's ideas but it was not until the mid-1940s that Walter Bird proposed, designed and manufactured an air-supported radome.[4] Ever since then, radomes have attracted the attention of architects because they make it possible to construct temporary coverings and portable buildings and to span large areas. However, they are limited to balloon-like structures.

Right

Floating theatre

The pneumatic floating theatre designed by
Murata and Kawaguchi was built for the
Electrical Industries Federation at EXPO' 70.
A PVC-coated double-woven polyester fabric
was draped over three large 3-metre-
diameter air-inflated arches. The fabric was
not the ceiling of the building. In order to
improve acoustics, a light polyester film was
attached to the undersides of the arches
and a slight negative pressure differential
between the inside of the film and the
interior provided a concave surface seen
from the interior. The pneumatic floating
theatre was one of the most advanced
inflatable structures of its time. Murata
has been awarded a special medal by the
Japanese Ministry of Science and
Technology to commemorate his work
on inflatable structures.

Opposite

Festo exhibition hall

An illustrative example of current high-tech
inflatable architecture is Festo's air-inflated
exhibition hall, designed by Rosemarie
Wagner, Axel Thallemer and Udo Rutsche.
It is constructed with a cubic interior
comprised of supporting structures built
with air-inflated chambers. The building
adapts itself to changing environmental
conditions using inflated elements. Even if
several chambers should fail, the
large number of relatively small ones ensures the
absolute stability of the building, which was
completely constructed and visualised via
computer. It comprises several inflatable
structural elements at a pressure of about
50 kPa, whereas the air pressure inside the
building is normal. Large inflated Hypalon-
coated polyester fabric beams act as
horizontal girders for the roof. Translucent
intermediate membranes connect the roof
girders and also function as skylights. The
negative pressure in the intermediate
membranes guarantees a stable roof
system.

An air-supported structure consists of a single membrane held in place by a relatively low pressure differential and differs from more conventional structural forms in that the membrane material does not directly resist the externally applied loads. The membrane is used to contain the internal volume of air, which in turn supports the applied loads. In theory, if the external loads were uniform and equal to the internal pressure, the membrane would just be a separating medium. In this case the membrane would be free of any tensile stress and the span of the air-supported structure would theoretically have no limit. In practice, however, the loading is never uniform and the internal pressure differential must be maintained at a higher level to be able to bear wind or snow loads, for example, on the structure. Air-supported structures are quite commonly used in architectural applications such as sports stadiums, swimming-pool enclosures, greenhouses and warehouses.

The pressure inside an air-supported structure is slightly above atmospheric pressure. Because people or vehicles are constantly coming into, or going out of, the structure, a constant supply of air is required to keep it at a satisfactory level. Special openings are usually incorporated in the building to maintain the pressure by simple fans or the wind. One could also think of creating an (additional) uplift force with hot air or lighter-than-air gases. Unlike in traditional architecture, an air-supported structure causes an uplift force instead of a weight that has to be distributed into the ground, and the anchorage forces have to be equally distributed in the membrane to avoid stress concentrations. Anchorage can be provided by ballast or by anchoring the air-supported structure directly to the ground, for example with a concrete foundation. Access openings are required for people or vehicles and, because of the slight overpressure inside the structure, loss of air will occur through these openings. Special provisions are required. The simplest access can be provided by a 'squeeze through' opening or a zip. More advanced solutions are counterbalanced or revolving doors, or the use of an airlock.

Air-inflated Structures

An air-supported structure has two major design problems: the provision of a continuous supply of air to maintain stability; and the prevention of excessive leakage of air. New air-inflated concepts were developed to overcome these problems. Air-inflated structures are more closely related than air-supported ones to more conventional structures.[5] Closed membrane sections are inflated to form structural elements like beams, columns, arches and walls. The load-bearing capacity of these is dependent on:

    the volume of air contained;
    the internal pressure level;
    the properties of the membrane material;
    the shape of the element;

Air-inflated structures can be further divided into the subcategories of tubular frame structures and dual-wall cushion ones. Tubular structures are made of a framework of inflated hoses under high pressure which often support a fabric membrane. The supported membrane can add considerably to the stability of the structure. Inflated dual-wall structures consist of two membrane walls, often connected by drop threads or diaphragms, under internal pressure. More complex shapes are possible with this type of construction.

The structural elements in air-inflated construction are self-contained. In architectural applications this means that the provision of special entrances, as in air-supported structures, is not required and that, because of the absence of an uplift force, an anchorage is only needed to withstand external loads like wind. Furthermore, because of the self-containment of the structural elements, in theory a constant air supply would not be necessary. It is, however, impossible to construct a completely airtight structure and a periodic replenishment of air (every three to six months) is usually needed. A constant air supply might be required for larger contained volumes of air. Temperature variations will cause

a change in pressure and air-inflated structures at a relatively low pressure may therefore require continuous pressure control. The effect of changes in temperature will be less pronounced where pressure is higher.

Initially air-inflated structures were more suitable for smaller spans. Bigger spans required higher pressures or large-diameter tubes, implying materials that were more airtight, and higher strength. Air-supported structures were more economical and structurally stable. Logically, hybrid concepts were developed to enhance the performance of inflatable structures. Hybrid structures can be subdivided into total pneumatic hybrids and partial pneumatic hybrids. Total pneumatic hybrid structures are a combination of air-supported and air-inflated structures. Large spans can be achieved by air-supported structures and insulation is added by dual-wall construction. Redundancy is introduced by combining the two different methods and therefore the risk of collapse is decreased. The introduction of more conventional types of construction yields a partially pneumatic hybrid structure. A good example is the semirigid airship, where a rigid keel is attached to the hull to relax the stresses in the envelope that result from bending.

Economic considerations and technology restraints, however, have forced manufacturers to concentrate on simple air-supported structures, implying cylindrical or spherical buildings of little aesthetic value. Various concepts for inflatable constructions have been exhibited at world expositions, leaving pneumatic structures with a mere curiosity value.

State-of-the- art Inflatable Architecture

The technological restraints in inflatable architecture

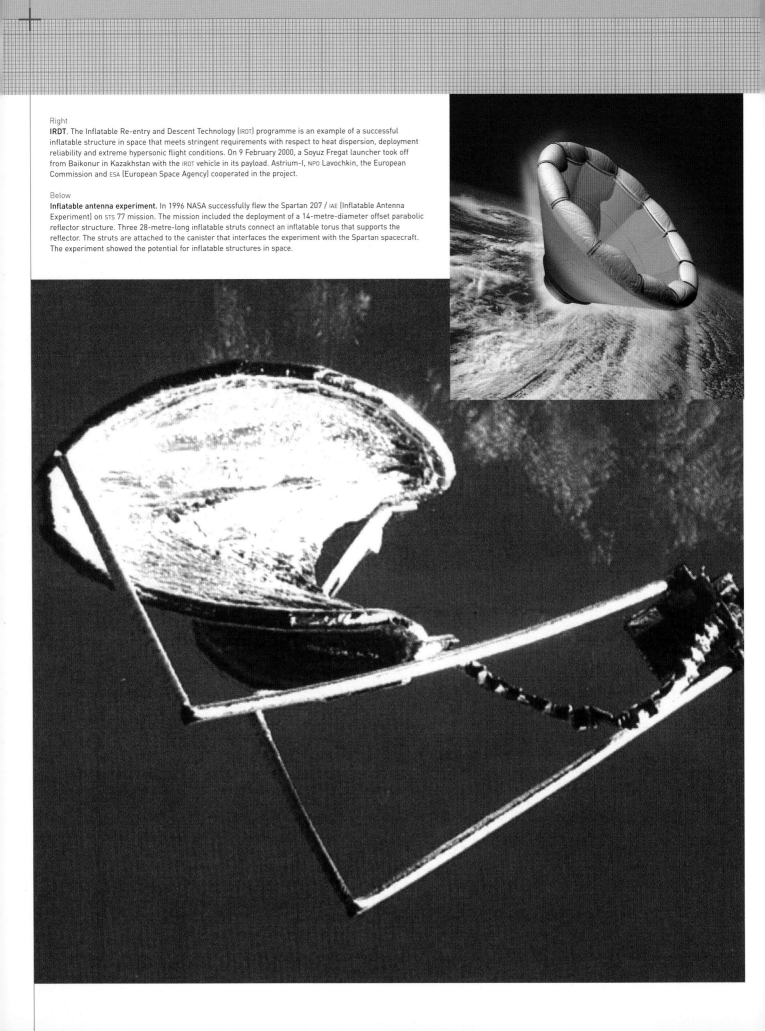

Right
IRDT. The Inflatable Re-entry and Descent Technology (IRDT) programme is an example of a successful inflatable structure in space that meets stringent requirements with respect to heat dispersion, deployment reliability and extreme hypersonic flight conditions. On 9 February 2000, a Soyuz Fregat launcher took off from Baikonur in Kazakhstan with the IRDT vehicle in its payload. Astrium-I, NPO Lavochkin, the European Commission and ESA (European Space Agency) cooperated in the project.

Below
Inflatable antenna experiment. In 1996 NASA successfully flew the Spartan 207 / IAE (Inflatable Antenna Experiment) on STS 77 mission. The mission included the deployment of a 14-metre-diameter offset parabolic reflector structure. Three 28-metre-long inflatable struts connect an inflatable torus that supports the reflector. The struts are attached to the canister that interfaces the experiment with the Spartan spacecraft. The experiment showed the potential for inflatable structures in space.

can now be solved by computer technology and the application of new advanced materials and manufacturing techniques. Traditional construction still dominates architectural engineering, but in this new millennium lightweight structures are being reconsidered. Technological advances allow for designs that break with the basic unattractive shapes and give way to novel, appealing concepts.

The army and other military and civilian organisations need large shelters that are transportable by air and can be rapidly erected in austere conditions. Wide-span shelters have a number of military and civilian uses, including vehicle and aircraft maintenance, disaster-relief material storage and personnel environmental shelter. New textile manufacturing technologies are being investigated to replace the aluminium or composite structures used for tent frames. Existing technologies involve adhesively bonding or welding together patterned, coated, flat-fabric goods to form an arch shape. Recent advances in high-pressure inflatable structures use a braiding process to fabricate seamless inflatable beams, or airbeams, and to make curved inflatable beams economically on straight mandrels. They are manufactured by continuously braiding or weaving a high-strength, three-dimensional fabric sleeve over an air-retention bladder. This technique provides for a seamless high-strength structure. By changing weave patterns, or adding different materials into the weave, the shape of the airbeam can be manipulated for use in many applications. It could also be used for space inflatables, temporary bridges and aircraft evacuation slides. Examples of this type of construction have been shown to be structurally efficient, robust and relatively economical. Airbeams with a span of up to 36 metres have been successfully demonstrated and ones with larger spans are currently under development.[6]

State-of-the-art Applications in Space

Recent years have seen a boom in the research into developing inflatable structures for use in space. This is primarily because of the four major advantages inflatable structures have over conventional rigid ones. They have low weight, low storage volume, are easy to deploy and their cost is low, resulting in much lower mission costs. Research focuses on five main applications: deceleration systems; antennae and reflectors; solar concentrators; rigidising support structures; and space habitats. The requirements for inflatable structures in space are much more stringent than those for architectural purposes. Hence, much can be learnt from surveys to design ultralightweight structures suitable for the space environment.

Research into inflatable structures for space applications focuses on deployment simulations and acquiring the required surface accuracy. For example, the surface accuracy of an inflatable antenna is in the order of millimetres, depending on the operating frequency.[8] Another example is an inflatable rigidisable support structure. A truss structure, consisting of inflatable tubes, is launched into space. In orbit the structure deploys by inflation. Once inflated, the skin material rigidifies and ensures that no further internal overpressure is necessary.[9]

This is important because this overpressure would make leakage unavoidable and would mean that a large amount of pressurised gas would be required for a long-term mission.

The Future of Lightweight Architecture

Lightweight architecture will play an important role in the near future. The shortage of oil reserves will redefine the way we design structures;[10] and the need to reduce energy consumption over the entire life span of a building will lead to the construction of lightweight structures such as inflatable ones. When mankind extends his domain into space, using inflatable structures will be the way to minimise energy consumption and hence mission costs. On earth, advanced computer programs developed for inflatable structures in space can be used to design new inflatable shapes. Rigidisable inflatable structures are the solution for relieving the pressure differential and will result in permanent structures. ⌂

Notes

1. A Beukers, E van Hinte, *Lightness: The inevitable renaissance of minimum energy structures*, 010 Publishers (Rotterdam), 1999, pp 137–8.
2. MF Ashby, *Materials Selection in Mechanical Design*, Pergamon Press (Oxford), 1992, p 3.
3. C Price, F Newby, RH Suan and FJ Samuely, *Air structures – A survey for the Department of the Environment*; commissioned by the Ministry of Public Building and Work, HMSO (London), 1971, p 5.
4. RN Dent, *Principles of Pneumatic Architecture*, The Architectural Press, (London), 1971, pp 34–5.
5. Ibid, p 17.
6. G Brown, R Haggard and B Norton, 'Inflatable structures for deployable wings', presented at the 42nd AIAA/ASME/ASCE/AHS/ASC Structures, Structural Dynamics, and Materials Conference & Exhibit, 16–19 April 2001, Seattle WA, AIAA paper 2001–68, p 21.
7. S L Veldman, Vermereen, C.A.J.R., *Inflatable structures in aerospace engineering - An overview*. Presented at the European conference on spacecraft structures, materials and mechanical testing, Noordwijk, the Netherlands 29 November – 1 December 2000, (ESA SP–468) pp 93-98.
8. CE Willey, RC Schulze, RS Bokulic, WE Skullney, JKH Lin, DP Cadogan and CF Knoll, 'A hybrid inflatable dish antenna system for spacecraft', presented at the 42nd Structures, Structural Dynamics, and Materials Conference & Exhibit, op cit, AIAA Paper 2001–1258, p 3.
9. D Cadogan and SE Scarborough, 'Rigidizable materials for use in gossamer space inflatable structures', presented at the 42nd Structures, Structural Dynamics, and Materials Conference & Exhibit, op cit, AIAA Paper 2001–1417, AIAA paper 2001–1417, pp 1–12.
10. A Beukers; *Minimum materials, maximum performance, maximum satisfaction*. In: Proceedings. Lightness (RAI Convention Centre, 11 November 2000), Doors of Perception, Amsterdam, 2000, pp 1–4.

This paper is inspired by Adriaan Beukers and Ed van Hinte, *Lightness: The inevitable renaissance of minimum energy structures*, 010 Publishers (Rotterdam), 1998. The authors of this paper are associate researchers at the Department of Production Technology of Delft University of Technology, Faculty of Aerospace Engineering. Professor Beukers is head of this department.

Below left
Mies in Berlin and Mies in America
Mies van der Rohe in his apartment on East Pearson Street, Chicago, 1964.
The exhibitions focusing on the two periods of Mies's career could be seen concurrently
in New York during the summer of 2001: 'Mies in Berlin' at MoMA and 'Mies in America'
at the Whitney Museum. Both shows are now touring internationally.

Below right
Ludwig van der Rohe in the garden of the Riehl
House, c1915 (Museum of Modern Art, New York:
Mies van der Rohe Archive).

Beat the Devil

During the entire summer and early autumn of 2001, New York exhibited an unprecedented preoccupation with architecture that was at once illuminating, overwhelming and total. All the major museums were unanimously dedicated to architectural exhibitions: 'Mies in Berlin' at the Museum of Modern Art, 'Mies in America' at the Whitney Museum and 'Frank Gehry, Architect' at the Solomon R Guggenheim Museum. In retrospect, after the architectural holocaust of 11 September, this stimulation of civic consciousness towards architecture and urbanism from June through to September can now be seen as prescient, haunting and necessary. Diane Lewis, one of the fifty international architects to be invited to the IIT Student Union competition to design an addition to the Mies Van der Rohe Campus and professor of architecture at Cooper Union, New York, describes how the discourse of the summer should be seen as a foundation for a new epoch – the examination of Mies being key.

It was only a week after the World Trade Center disaster that I interviewed Terence Riley, chief curator of architecture and design at the Museum of Modern Art and co-curator of the Mies van der Rohe exhibition at the museum. The sense of shock was still evident and the city visibly shaken.

A new appetite for the existential power and directness of a Miesian ability to integrate the contemporary with the historic – its role in the fabric and programme of the American city best demonstrated in the Seagram Plaza in New York, the Federal Plaza in Chicago and the Dominion Center in Toronto – has emerged. Sharpened by the events of 11 September, Mies's architectural urbanism has become consciously appreciated over the last few years as a potent antidote to Post-Modernism, before which the oeuvre of Mies was often regarded as a Utopic formalist approach. Riley feels that 'The Post-Modern, with its promise of the restoration and reconstruction of the traditional city without the loss of the benefits of modern life and its technologies, was an alluring prospect in the 1970s and 1980s – one which the general public may or may not have believed in. However, its inability to deliver this promise became evident as the outcome of Battery Park, the Seaside projects and Disney unfolded. It may have been possible for Post-Modernism to rehabilitate Louis Kahn (in spite of his clear allegiance to the Modern Movement) because of his roots in the Beaux Arts, but it could not do the same for Mies who remained the undeniable ground zero of

the movement'. A reluctance, even inability, to return to the promise of the Post-Modern has silenced its voices and has prompted a broad acceptance of Mies's contribution. The Miesian terrain has thus become more understandable and, in doing so, has shifted position to again being essential to contemporary discourse on the relation of form and content. The possibilities spawned for the architecture of the city have proved even more charged and profound within the European/American juxtapositions that the two exhibitions – 'Mies in Berlin' at the Museum of Modern Art and 'Mies in America' at the Whitney Museum – have presented.

The exhibitions have, furthermore, marked the end of a historical era for MoMA, during which Philip Johnson and Henry-Russell Hitchcock were the main authorities on the subject of Mies. (Mies was first brought to prominence in America by Johnson and Hitchcock's seminal 1932 'Modern Architecture: International Exhibition' and Johnson continued to champion him at MoMA throughout the 1930s, 1940s and early 1950s during the periods when he was curator of architecture at the museum.) In the 'Mies in Berlin' exhibition the issues surrounding Mies, the Second World War and the postwar dialogue between the architects of Europe and the US, discussion of which

had previously been guarded, were newly represented by exquisite archival research from the Mies archives in MoMA. Additional works were also mined from international resources by Terence Riley and his co-curator Barry Bergdoll, professor of art history at Columbia University. The new criticality was further emphasised by the exhibition being shown in conjunction with 'Mies in America', literally down the road at the Whitney. The decision to divide the subject matter between the two museums became the poignant articulation of difference through which this new examination was undertaken. The simultaneous Gehry retrospective, across the park at the Guggenheim, was consciously positioned as a historical counterpoint – a conversation between 'masters'.

At the press conference for 'Mies in Berlin' Riley referred to the exhibition as a 'revision', in the sense that it was a generational change of interpretation which, with the exception of a few elements, could be understood as progressively putting Mies into context. In the catalogue the curators note Mies's statement that an exhibition 'must bring about a revolution in our thinking'. Their scholarly work (and that of the contributors to the catalogue) has resulted in a text 'intrinsic' to Mies's work: an exquisite succession of drawings, project histories, photographs and philosophically related works by his artist comrades. Referring to the way Mies was presented in Johnson and Hitchock's 1932 exhibition and International Style book, Riley explains in the catalogue that: 'Johnson's and Mies' efforts were complementary but not equivalent ... Johnson's book aspired to a traditional art historical narrative, Mies' "text" though not a text in the traditional sense had its own message.' The curators' reading of that 'text' is reflected in the structure of the exhibition, which contains a genealogy of the architect's precedents beginning with Schinkel's Charlottenhof and Roman Bath at Potsdam.

This new climate of reconsideration, coupled with the desire for a politically 'unexpurgated' view of the Modern Movement, was established by the decision to exhibit Mies's previously taboo designs for the Rosa Luxemburg monument; he first proposed the project as a major photo mural for his first show, 'Mies van der Rohe', at MoMA in 1947. During our interview, Terence Riley revealed that Mies's proposal to exhibit the mural after the war caused considerable dissent in the museum, with curators protesting and withdrawing. Riley describes the limitations on past examinations of the Modern Movement, and particularly Mies van der Rohe, as the 'packaging of the European work for exportation to the United States'. He also brought to my attention the irony in choosing Mies for the subject of an exhibition that was the first of its kind in New York after the end of the Second World War. This was only compounded by omitting to mention that Germany was Mies's place of birth.

During the summer of 2001 Mies in New York was revealed in a new form, not only in the context of MoMA – the museum that gave him to us in the mid-20th century. At the Whitney, an important incarnation of Miesian space was generated by Mies artefacts within Marcel Breuer's museum. However, the two exhibitions had dramatically different approaches. MoMA's 'Mies in Berlin' was linear, literary and scholarly, while the 'Mies in America' show was a visceral architectural experience, in the form of its installation and in its commissioned video works. Combined, the scope of the material the two exhibitions covered illuminated Mies's life and work to a new degree, with a refreshing image of its continuity and a refined expression of its integrity.

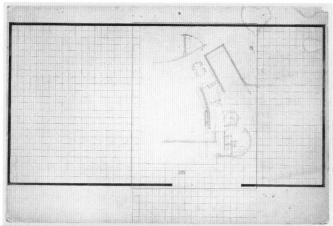

Whereas the exhibition reassessing Mies's early work in Berlin was organised by two professional academics, Terence Riley and Barry Bergdoll, his American career was curated by the architect Phyllis Lambert with the aid of a Whitney curator and Harvard professor, K Michael Hays, who helped to organise the venue. The founder and director of the Canadian Center for Architecture, Lambert was also the client who selected Mies to design the Seagram Building.

The use in the Whitney exhibition of the Phyllis Lambert archives – the collection of the instrumental eyewitness – crucially supported the new implications of Mies's career as excavated from the MoMA archives and international resources. The museum presented him in a 'one-man show' with careful architectural authenticity. Unadulterated, syncopated and magnetic, the spatially taut-free plan installation captured the mental character of his work with a haunting audio accompaniment. Installed in the cavernous masonry monumentality of Breuer's stone floors and concrete ceiling-grid, each element was imbued with the character of the suspended works of art in Mies's own Convention Center collages. For it seems that Lambert was intent on finally telling the story of Mies in America from her own perspective. This included this truly powerful installation of an authentic ambience, an ambience related to the surrounding Breuer building. Thus her project was to successfully embody the work in all its texture, spatiality, tectonic clarity, philosophic nuance and artistic collegiality. This necessitated the brilliant inclusion of the original editions of the books which most influenced his thinking, the paintings he collected from the

colleagues he spoke to ideologically and intellectually, and the collages he made that integrated works from a vast knowledge of the history of civilisation. In line with this, Lambert specially commissioned the artist Inigo Manglano-Ovalle to make the haunting magnetised video of the Neue Nationalgalerie, the Federal Plaza and the Seagram Building. These are shot from a precise eye-level camera with the purist conception of the constant observer – the movement beyond what is permanent or ephemeral. A work that is philosophically continuous with the inner structure of Mies's thinking.

The exhibition at the Whitney so powerfully captured continuity of thought and ambience that these combined to snatch a glimpse of memories of the beat generation in New York. For it was an ambience that was deeply effective through the means of abstraction, actual materiality, conceptual structure, photography and powerful opacities of primary colour - the material of the works themselves. It was in Mies's mould, a beauty derived from truth. Mies beat the devil. Once in New York, once in Berlin. The vision of the glass skyscraper transposed urbanist innovations from the Unter den Linden and Friedrichstrasse of Berlin into the urban text of Park Avenue. His return to Berlin in the 1960s to realise a temple and crypt to house the art of the resistance to fascism on the rubble of Speer's totalitarian axis is the Neue Nationalgalerie. In German it is said that the devil is in the detail; 'God is in the details', has been attributed to both Flaubert and Mies.

The dialogue achieved between the two Mies exhibitions demonstrated the interaction between the Berlin projects and their manifestations in America, particularly New York. As stated before, the Seagram Building is clearly the realisation on Park Avenue of the concepts of the glass skyscraper of the Friedrichstrasse. The early drawings of the Seagram proved so influential that other architects often inherited the concretising of imagery. A clear example of a literal realisation of a powerful drawing, constructed by strong charcoal verticals, is the austere elevation of the flat-topped glass skyscraper that can easily be recognised in form and texture as Eero Saarinen's CBS Tower on 53rd Street.

At this distance from the visionary imagery of Mies's Berlin projects, the role of New York between the two world wars, as the protector of the architectural avant-garde of Europe and a refuge for those who aspired to the humanist post-monarchical programme of the Modern Movement, is more palpable. The artists and architects who comprised the intellectual resistance were re-engaged in the city, which profited from the erudition that Gropius, Mies and Breuer rescued from the European rubble. New York, which was strongly receptive to Miesian style during the 1950s and 1960s,

thus brought radical buildings to fruition. The current climate of critique provoked by the exhibitions at MoMA and the Whitney has revealed the nature of the liberal forces that were at work in the city and in America, which were necessary to the realisation of so many seminal ideas – and has also revealed those who were opposed to them.

This reconsideration of the implementation of Modern Movement principles of structure and urbanism, adopted during the postwar era with the realisation of the Seagram Building, the Whitney and Guggenheim museums and Lever House, is also crucial to the challenge that the Gehry exhibition at the Guggenheim attempted to present. Within the pervasive presence of Mies at the other museums, it drew a historical continuity between Frank Gehry and Frank Lloyd Wright. In the catalogue for the exhibition the comparison to Wright was emphasised through the introductory model and drawings for Gehry's future waterfront Guggenheim in New York. The project was advocated as a historical parallel to the original Guggenheim by Wright, and was described as requiring a similarly powerful community vision for its advancement. As an introduction to his total oeuvre, Gehry proposes how New York can reinstate a radical, informed and participatory architectural urbanism. The argumentation inspired by these exhibitions, particularly by Phyllis Lambert's perspective on Mies, has renewed a vision of New York's postwar political and architectural history which may finally succeed in liberating our discourse from the shackles of the false opposition between history and contemporaneity with which the International Style vision of the Modern Movement had imprisoned the city, with the result that during the Post-Modern era, dating from 1978, considerations of style above idea and social content usurped the type of thinking represented in these exhibitions.

In looking at Mies in a postwar context, his relationship with history cannot be overlooked. However, the often-repeated accusations of his political acquiescence to the Nazi regime cannot be clarified or proven or disproven. One has to read his motives in his language – spoken, written and architectural – and in one's own experience, if any, of survival and activism in the theatre of war.

His courage and interest in constructing the convention centre photomontage/collages which confront the issues of mass psychology are an extraordinary silent testimony to the issues confronting Mies's psyche in the postwar United States. The exquisite field condition of the 300 foot span space frame under which is collaged a range of physical images from photographic crowds confronted with the American flag, to abstract works of art, to Buddha; these are a contemplative demonstration of the possibilites of civic gathering, peacefulness, perhaps his appreciation and understanding of the possibilities of Jeffersonian democracy after the experience of the rallies of prewar Germany. They are profoundly moving punctuations within the work in the Whitney exhibition.

During our conversation, Riley agreed with my comparison of Mies with the posture of Thomas Mann's narrator in *Dr Faustus* – the artist from a deteriorating fascist society who is at once an opponent and a member of it, and who tries to take responsibility for each of his actions. Mies stated: 'Our era is no better nor worse than any other. The value is how one asserts oneself in the face of circumstance.'

Riley pointed out that Mies's father, who is often described as a stonecutter, was probably merely the maker of petit-bourgeois gravestones and that the stonework which Mies supposedly learnt might well have been that of the graveyard. The craft he may have learned was that of the simple act of carving of the name of the dead on each stone. The Spenglerian sense of life and death penetrates every aspect of his architecture. That is very much the sense necessary to the architecture of New York today. ⅅ

The Gehry and Mies exhibitions are currently touring internationally: 'Mies in Berlin' is at the Altes Museum, Berlin, from 14 December 2001 to March 2002 and at the Fundacio la Caixa, Barcelona, from 30 July to 29 September 2002; 'Mies in America' is at the Canadian Centre for Architecture, Montreal, from 17 October 2001 to 20 January 2002; 'Frank Gehry, Architect' is at the Guggenheim Museum Bilbao from 29 October 2001 to 3 February 2002.

Below main
Site plan: The Climate Prediction Center is located on the Lamont Doherty earth observatory campus of Columbia University, up the Hudson River valley from New York City. After its completion, Rafael Viñoly was asked to develop a masterplan for the whole campus.

Below inset
From the approach the new single-storey building does not obscure the expansive view of the river. Stone for the wall was sourced locally, adding to the affinities between building and site.

Climate Prediction Center

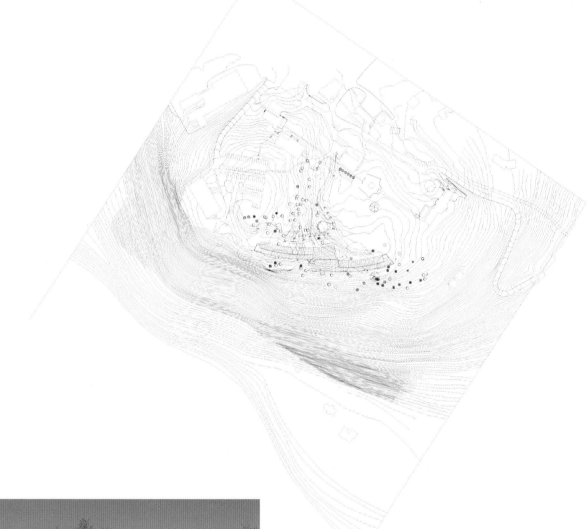

Jeremy Melvin looks at a seemingly humble and economical building for Columbia University by Rafael Viñoly Architects that has pragmatically taken its prompts from its beautiful site high on a cliff overlooking the Hudson River.

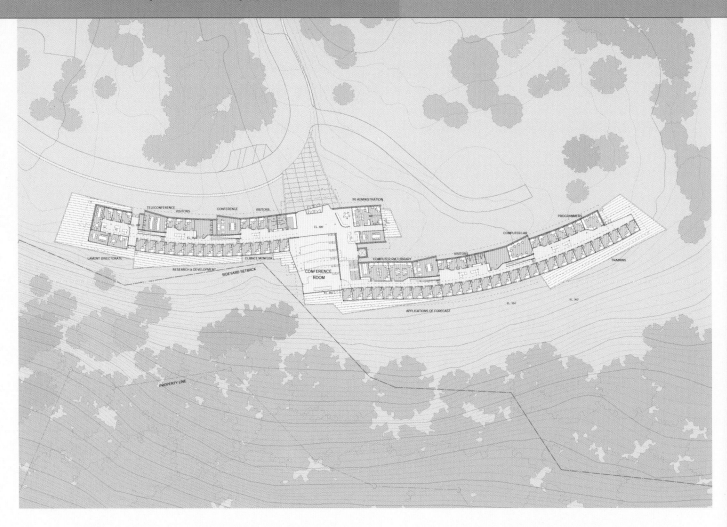

'These are the people who define the theory of El Nino,' says Rafael Viñoly of the users of his Climate Prediction Center at Columbia University's earth observatory campus overlooking the Hudson River some 45 miles north of New York City. Hugging the contours of its spectacular site, this long, low building houses a group of multidisciplinary researchers who look at the 'legal, health, cultural and scientific aspects' of the 'whole phenomenon of deep water heating in the Pacific'. The centre, a joint programme between the US Federal Government and Columbia University, arose from the aim of turning long-range weather forecasting into policy formation and implementation, and has grown into an international research centre with input from 68 countries. Its companion departments on the Lamont Doherty campus are seismology, marine biology, geophysics, terrestrial geology, petrology, geochemistry, oceanography and palaeontology, with a total of 430 staff.

Explaining how he, best known for urban buildings such as the Tokyo International Forum, tackled a rural site, Viñoly explains, 'There's little profit in dissociating each commission from its origins ... each is site-, moment- and programme-specific'. The specifics of a site, not different sensibilities applied to rural and urban locations, drive his design approach, and here they are spectacular. High on a cliff overlooking an

expanse of the Hudson valley, the site's remarkable natural beauty has attracted some of New York's wealthiest people for several hundred years. Columbia's campus was itself a private 149-acre estate, reworked by Frederick Law Olmsted's son with a formal garden at its heart, before it was left to the university. Understandably 'neighbourhood control', with the Rockefellers close by and exercised through the Hudson Preservation Group, is strong. But it was Viñoly himself, when interviewed for the Climate Prediction Center, who derided the existing site masterplan for a series of independent buildings as being inappropriate to the setting and undermining of the programme because it was 'not going to foster interaction'.

Instead he proposed a single-storey, ground-hugging building of two gently curving wings which overlap to form a central node. From the opposite bank it resembles a thin blade poised between the ground and tree line. Its approach is from the land side, and it appears first as a low stone wall under a shallow-curved metal-clad roof, but on entering into the node the view across the magnificent landscape opens. Generous and amply lit, with a descending staircase to the lower wing, the node serves as a meeting space

Below top
The generous volume and abundant natural light in the entrance area encourage lingering
and create the backdrop for informal gatherings, break-out sessions from the lecture room
and evening cocktails. Using standard timber components kept costs low but did not preclude
quite complex forms, and gives the building an air of a particular strand of rural American
domestic architecture.

Below bottom
Typical section: Customising simple, cheap, mass-produced components
gave a basic form of a centrally loaded corridor; researchers' rooms
overlook the view with computers and services to the rear. The roof
form, opening windows and the central clerestory assist ventilation and
bring light into the centre of the plan.

115+

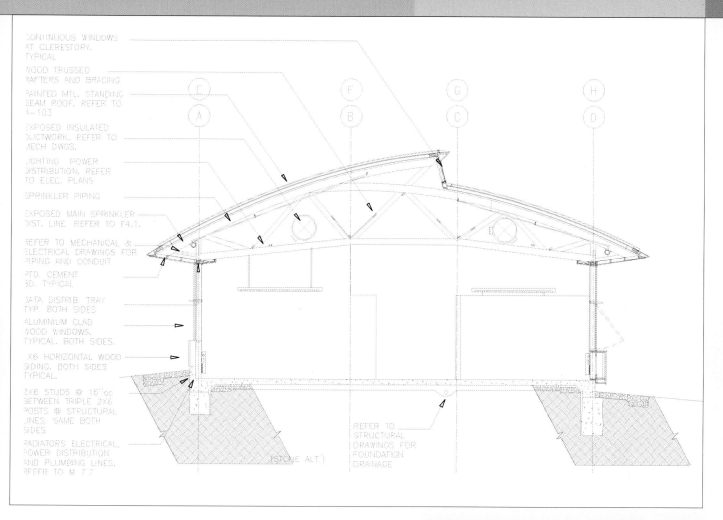

CONTINUOUS WINDOWS
AT CLERESTORY.
TYPICAL

WOOD TRUSSED
RAFTERS AND BRACING

PAINTED MTL. STANDING
SEAM ROOF. REFER TO
A-103

EXPOSED INSULATED
DUCTWORK. REFER TO
MECH DWGS.

LIGHTING POWER
DISTRIBUTION. REFER
TO ELEC. PLANS

SPRINKLER PIPING

EXPOSED MAIN SPRINKLER
DIST. LINE. REFER TO F4.1.

REFER TO MECHANICAL &
ELECTRICAL DRAWINGS FOR
PIPING AND CONDUIT

PTD. CEMENT
BD. TYPICAL

DATA DISTRIB TRAY
TYP. BOTH SIDES

ALUMINIUM CLAD
WOOD WINDOWS.
TYPICAL. BOTH SIDES.

X6 HORIZONTAL WOOD
SIDING. BOTH SIDES
TYPICAL.

2X6 STUDS @ 16"oc
BETWEEN TRIPLE 2X6
POSTS @ STRUCTURAL
LINES. SAME BOTH
SIDES

RADIATORS ELECTRICAL
POWER DISTRIBUTION
AND PLUMBING LINES.
REFER TO M 7.2

(STONE ALT)

REFER TO
STRUCTURAL
DRAWINGS FOR
FOUNDATION
DRAINAGE

which apparently comes to life at an early evening 'happy
hour', and has a lecture room adjacent to the main entrance.
This facility, with 200 seats, can be used by people from across
the campus. Wide corridors, also allowing for interaction, lead
into the two wings. On one side, overlooking the view, are the
individual rooms where the researchers work; on the other
side, encased in the fieldstone wall, are the supercomputers
that crunch the data from which their predictions might turn
into the foundations of policy. As researchers work with data
rather than lethal viruses or nuclear material, the specific
performance standards are less exacting and the scope for
architecture, as a stimulus to imaginative and creative
interpretation and analysis, is perhaps greater.

Keeping the form and construction simple had another
benefit: cost. As Viñoly says, the university did 'not have
enough money' to construct a conventional research building.
Using a single-storey structure 'eliminated elevators, reduces
fireproofing and kept it simple', all significantly reducing
expense. The relatively narrow width of the wing allows for
natural ventilation 'to shorten the [artificial] cooling season',
while the roof form assists natural airflow and provides a
clerestory for light and extraction along the length of the
building. Moreover, the architects identified basic construction
systems, from 'very cheap, simple housing', where there are

Below bottom
A lecture room with 200 seats provides for formal presentations of research findings. The apparently 'low tech' timber construction conceals sophisticated imaging and audio technology – including facilities for simultaneous translation, a useful attribute for a centre which draws on input from 68 countries.

Below top
Section through main stair: The entrance is at the central node, which becomes a space for formal and informal interaction, with a lecture room at the upper, entrance level and a stair to the lower wing.

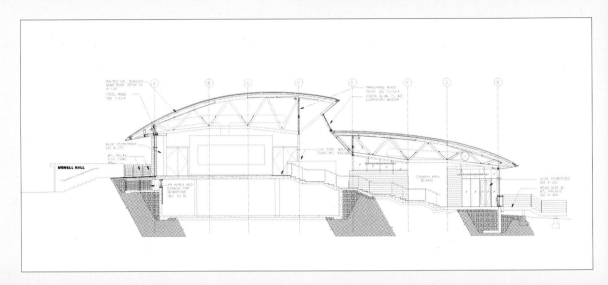

Below top
Aerial view: On the edge of the steep gorge down to the river, the Climate Prediction Center marks a point where the cultivated landscape of the campus gives way to wild and elemental natural scenery.

Below bottom inset
Sketch: The long, low building sits just above the cliff top and below the tree line.

'large manufacturers of simple trusses, prefabricated' with multiple nails to join them together rather than elaborate connections. On site all that was necessary was 'to bang in the nails'. Timber and stone both come from the immediate grounds, and the technology was well within the compass of local builders. By 'using off-the-shelf products we were able to deliver to the university,' explains Viñoly, and the character and construction of these lend the building an air of that tradition of American domestic architecture where timber structures make bright and airy spaces.

With the site topography establishing the building's form, and local materials providing its components, the centre's design is, in Viñoly's phrase, 'self-determined'. Such connections with locality might suggest an affinity between construction and programme – a 'sustainable' building housing a community that studies climate change or the effect of nonsustainable pursuits – but his contact with the research carried out at the centre makes Viñoly sceptical of easy references. This is not 'a Greenpeace type of building,' he says. 'It is remarkable how much of this ideology is politically tainted', with selective promotion of apparently environmental policies for other ends. Referring obliquely to his clients' work, he remarks that 'there are huge areas people don't know about', which by implication might have far more dramatic effects than others that are in popular currency.

In resisting the temptation to design an overly didactic building whose embodied 'sustainability' would direct the formulation of broader policies on the subject, Viñoly shows an appreciation of the limits of architecture. By concentrating on the pragmatic and the knowable, though, the design suggests a deeper affinity with academic work than a simplistically didactic building would have done. Serious research, too, has to focus on what can be known and proven; and if the points it uncovers are to feed into policy they must be pragmatic. Here the design provides, within the framework set by development control and cost, a facility to support research – the technology, and the spaces for working and for formal and informal interaction. Beyond that, the building becomes mute and the intellectual product of its users takes over.

From his initial perceptions about the failings of the existing masterplan to develop the Climate Prediction Center design, Viñoly set a new pattern for the campus. This continues in work on a new masterplan which aims to use the disciplines of construction, cost and development control, and topography of the site to incorporate climate prediction's companion disciplines, setting a strategy for the evolution of earth sciences and the interaction between the different components. ⚏

S333

Lucy Bullivant profiles a young international practice featured in the British Council's exhibition 'Space Invaders', who originally formed in London and have since made their base in the Netherlands where they are completing their first major project at the CiBoGa Terrain in Groningen.

Below opposite
Aerial perspective.

Below
Axonometric illustrating organisational layering

Below top
Model shot.

Below bottom
Plan.

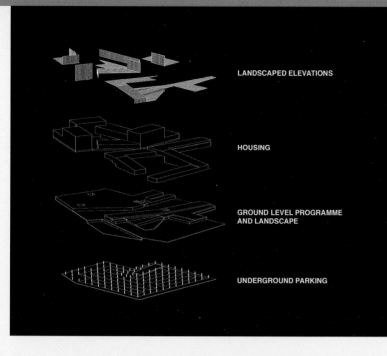

LANDSCAPED ELEVATIONS

HOUSING

GROUND LEVEL PROGRAMME
AND LANDSCAPE

UNDERGROUND PARKING

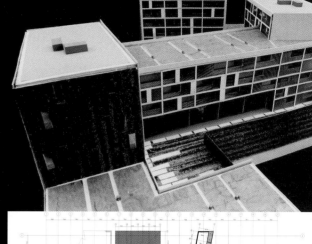

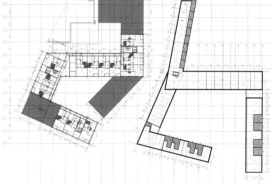

Schots 1 and 2, **CiBoGa Terrain, Groningen, the Netherlands, 1997–2002**
In this first phase of CiBoGa Terrain's housing development, S333 create a strategic link
through the city's ecological corridor, connecting the canal with an existing urban park
and the city centre with 20th-century housing extensions. S333 is currently building
Schots 1 and 2, the first of 13 compact buildings to be distributed across the site in an
open landscape designed by Will Alsop. At street level are shops. Above, Schots 1, clad
in an array of different glass panels, has a variety of open and semi-open collective spaces
including a winter garden intersected by a gallery to the apartments. The housing at Schots
2, clad in darkly stained western red cedar, is accessed by a sloping ground surface.
Landscape is interwoven as a planemetric layer with the architecture.

S333 is a multinational studio of architects and urbanists,
based in Amsterdam. It considers the nature of practice to be
the single most critical question for architecture today. Without
being self-conscious or overly academic, S333 has found a
method of working that gives it an essential edge. Rather than
representing the purely physical, it is committed to seeking out
effective operating strategies. Part of the office's practical
reflection includes finding ways to bring architecture,
landscape, socioeconomics and urbanism closer together. It is
a mode of experimentation that seeks to 'immerse'
architecture within contemporary cultural conditions. Thus
S333 can be seen to embody what can be regarded as a slow
paradigm shift in architecture. Insufficiently acknowledged,
perhaps because of its global fragmentation, this shift does
nevertheless represent a new vision of planning. Given the
opportunity, the architects enter the design process earlier
than normal, shifting the client's emphasis from solving
singular problems to searching for the right questions.

S333 has been located in Amsterdam since 1997 when the
practice moved to the Dutch capital in order to build the first
phase of the CiBoGa Terrain – a major housing commission,
currently under construction, which it won through the
Europan 3 competition. The office's partners are a multi-

national team: Dominic Papa and Jonathan Woodroffe
are British, Burton Hamfelt is Canadian and
Christopher Moller is a New Zealander. All four have
forged important links in a Dutch–British network that
includes the former bosses of three of them: Wiel Arets
and Farrell (Dominic Papa), Neutelings Riedijk
(Jonathan Woodroffe and Burton Hamfelt) and Xaveer
de Geyter (Hamfelt). Christopher Moller is also a part-
time senior urban planner for the city of Groningen,
while all four have links with the Architectural
Association in London – Papa and Woodroffe have run
Intermediate Unit 9 for the last 4 years, Moller is tutor
in the housing and urbanism unit, and Hamfelt is a
visiting critic.

S333's earliest work as a loose collaborative in
London under the name Studio 333, focused on
competitions, workshops and publications, mainly as a
means of generating debate about contemporary
European urbanism. Intentionally staying small and
mobile in order to respond quickly and effectively in a
variety of situations, S333 has evolved more in the
direction of an organisation than as a standard
architectural office. The partners refer to themselves as

Below
Organisational Chart

Below top
Diagram demonstrating S333's proposal for a park that superimposes 'cultural', 'extensive' and 'intensive' bands.

Below bottom
Organisational perspective.

gouden DRIEHOEK

PROGRAMMA	FUNCTIE	BESTAANDE	VOORSTEL	GLOBAAL	REGIONAAL	LOCAAL	4 SEASONS	OPEN	OPENBARE	PRIVEE	BAND
ANIMAL FARM	RECREATIE		●		●	●	4	24	X	X	EXTENSIVE
AURAL OASIS	PARK		○		●	●	4	12	X	X	NETWORK
BIGSPOTTERS HILL	RECREATIE	○		●			3	18	X		INTENSIVE
BLOEMMARKT	CULTUUR		○		●		4	9		X	NETWORK
BRAINSTORM PARK HOTEL	RECREATIE		●				4	24		X	INTENSIVE
CLUB HOUSE	RECREATIE	○				●	4	12		X	NETWORK
COUNTRY ESTATES	LUXE WONINGBOUW		○			●	4	24		X	EXTENSIVE
DRIVE-IN CINEMA	RECREATIE		○		●	●	1	3		X	NETWORK
EVENT SPACE	GROEN		○		●	●	1	-	X	X	NETWORK
FIETS HUUR/WINKEL	RECREATIE		○		●	●	2	12		X	NETWORK
FOG FOREST	PARK		○			●	2	12	X		NETWORK
FORT VIJFHUIZEN	CULTUUR	○		●	●		3	9	X		NETWORK
GOLF COURSE	RECREATIE	○			●	●	4	12	X		
HORECA	PARK		○		●	●	4	12	X		
HISTORISCH MUSEUM HAARLEMMERMEER	CULTUUR	○		●	●		4	9	X		NETWORK
MISSISSIPPI BOAT RIDE	RECREATIE		○	●	●		4	9		X	NETWORK
MUSEUM CRUQUIUS	CULTUUR	○		●	●		4	9	X		NETWORK
MANEGE	RECREATIE		○	●	●		4	12			EXTENSIVE
OPENLUCHT TONEEL	PARK		○	●	●		2	9		X	EXTENSIVE
PARK ENTREE	PARK		○	●	●		4	24	X		NETWORK
RUCKRIEM PAVILLION	CULTUUR		○	●	●		4	-	X		NETWORK
SPORTEN VELD	RECREATIE		○	●	●		4	12	X	X	EXTENSIVE
TALKING TREES	GROEN		○	●	●		2	12	X		NETWORK
THE WET	CULTUUR		○	●	●		4	12	X	X	INTENSIVE
TREE HOUSES	LUXE WONINGBOUW		○			●	4	24		X	EXTENSIVE

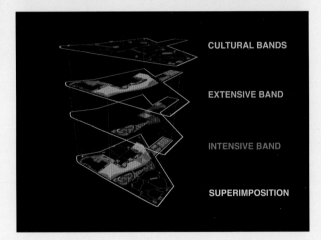

CULTURAL BANDS

EXTENSIVE BAND

INTENSIVE BAND

SUPERIMPOSITION

Flowing Park City, Haarlemmermeer, the Netherlands
S333 responded to the brief to create a new park identity, taking advantage of the spatial, cultural and historic qualities of the site, by speculating on a new type of park and city. This mixes fast and slow programmes, loud and quiet events, mobile visitors and permanent dwellers. Three main activity bands – one intensive, several extensive bands and a cultural network band – fit within the existing landscape. The intensive band stimulates day tourism, and is car-based; the extensive band implements slow activities like golf, water trips, new forests and animal parks; the cultural network joins a museum, an open-air theatre and a sculpture park by a series of continuous pathways.

'space directors' rather than designers of space: 'We are interested in how you grow a piece of city and then how you build it.' Their projects go beyond the physical limits of a site, showing how scale can dramatically reconfigure context and broaden the experience of a programme. Urban form, they say, is not an inward looking 'puzzle typology in a box'. Consultants to Dutch local governments as well as to private clients, as architects they talk in a more popular idiom.

It was a topological transformation rather than a building that brought S333 to wider public attention. Commissioned by the city of Zaanstad in the Netherlands, their project 'Dutch Mountain' (1997) transformed a 4-hectare waste dump into a recreational park that incorporates Land Art. The park gave S333 the ideal opportunity to preach not only variety of forms but also the potential of context. When it comes to housing, the office has also been working mainly in a Dutch context: the notable exceptions are its UK schemes for Toynbee Housing Association at Tarling in East London and its prize-winning Europan 4 scheme for the city of Manchester. The two blocks for the CiBoGa Terrain in Groningen, a city in the north of the Netherlands known for its innovative urban developments, is the office's *pièce de résistance*. This first phase of CiBoGa has been on site since 1999 and is due for completion in the spring of 2002. (S333's involvement with the project has been long term – the office has been working with the city of Groningen on the planning of this large-scale housing scheme since 1994.) Consisting of 13 compact housing blocks in all, on a 6-hectare site, the projected completion date is not until at least 2010. For this first phase though, the architects have created what they refer to as Schots ('ice blocks' in Dutch) – two building blocks that are sculpted by movement flows, sight lines and open public spaces. These are overlaid by the landscape which interweaves with the architecture to promote biodiversity. Different types of glass and wood panels which change colour and texture over time have been chosen. All around these facades are gardens, patios, ramped surfaces, courtyards and playgrounds.

Flowing Park City is S333's entry for an invited competition for post-Floriade 2002 redevelopment. An international garden festival, it is to be held in the midst of a 240-hectare landscaped park on the Haarlemmermeer polder. Acknowledging that to keep such a park in divine isolation no longer works, S333 entered a speculative design for a small- and large-scale park and tourist facilities, and cultural and

recreational activities. It aims to create a 'fast and slow' park/city programme in which different worlds can mingle with one another: the park and tourist facilities, cultural and recreational activities. These are combined in three activity bands – 'extensive', 'intensive' and 'cultural network' – that offer a mix of loud and quiet events for visitors and local inhabitants. The design breaks down the the traditionally strong definitions of park and city, and merges them through an awareness of seasonal and daily patterns of use. The large flat location, which borders the Ringvaart canal and is divided by the new N22 highway, has been slowly colonised for a range of purposes.

Another project where the site is perceived as an 'urban ecology' is La Ville Forêt, an urban transformation scheme for the city of Grenoble in France. The result of an invited competition, it establishes a set of programmatic layers that create a new density and a flexible blueprint for a future community. Competing for people presents future challenges for this city, therefore the problem of an exodus to the suburbs, which brings with it urban sprawl without real growth, is reconfigured. Whereas tall housing blocks (1,700 units) bring generous views of the surrounding mountains, this is counterbalanced at ground level by a diversity of

programme: car-parking areas, collective and private gardens, and leisure and retail facilities are innovatively stacked as related facilities. Here S333's interest in manipulating programme to create a sense of place treats form as a verb, injecting architecture with a clear organisational creativity. ⌀

Further work by S333 can be viewed on their website: www. s333.org
Space Invaders: emerging UK architecture is a new international touring exhibition mounted by the British Council's Art Architecture and Design Department. It explores the expanding social identity of architecture and the cultural strategies that enhance its relationship with everyday life. The exhibition, which opened in Lisbon in the autumn of 2001, tours this year to Berlin, Warsaw, Prague, Tallinn and Los Angeles.

It features fifteen of the UK's most innovative and culturally informed architectural practices. This emerging generation is intent on extending the concept of architecture. Besides S333, the architects included are David Adjaye, atopia, Block, dECOI, drmm (de Rijke Marsh Morgan), East, FAT, Foreign Office Architecture (FOA), General Lighting and Power (GLP) Klein Dytham Architects (KDa), muf, Piercy Conner, softroom and Urban Salon. Lucy Bullivant has curated the exhibition with Pedro Gadanho, an architect, and the project includes a two hour film of interviews made by Lucy with location footage directed by Elliott Chaffer of Milk. Current tour details are available via the Art Architecture and Design section of the British Council's website: www.britishcouncil.org

Below top and middle
Computer renderings of the block's interior.

Below bottom
Colonising block.

Below bottom
Model.

La Ville Forêt, Grenoble, France
La Ville Forêt (the urban forest) is an attempt to grow an existing city, increasing its size and activities vertically in combination with a smaller scale colonisation of the ground. The project is best understood as an 'urban ecology' with seven organising layers or urban tools (see illustration) designed to produce a critical mass and density for the site, and a *growth strategy* for the city. The project features a diversity of housing typologies, and stacked parking, public and private gardens offering a landscape of views as a competitive alternative to the lure of the suburban house on the facing mountains.

Below top
Colonising block.

Below middle
Sections of the housing blocks, revealing the layering of its programme.

Below bottom
Diagram illustrating the relation between site and landscapes of mobility.

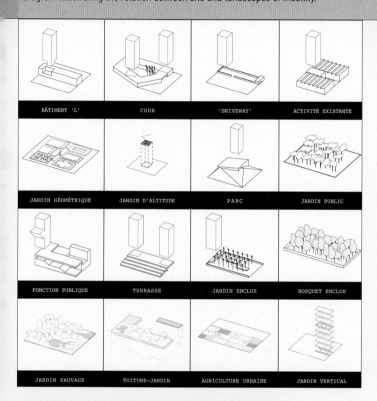

BÂTIMENT 'L' | COUR | 'DRIVEWAY' | ACTIVITÉ EXISTANTE
JARDIN GÉOMÉTRIQUE | JARDIN D'ALTITUDE | PARC | JARDIN PUBLIC
FONCTION PUBLIQUE | TERRASSE | JARDIN ENCLOS | BOSQUET ENCLOS
JARDIN SAUVAGE | TOITURE-JARDIN | AGRICULTURE URBAINE | JARDIN VERTICAL

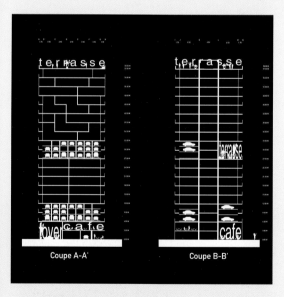

Coupe A-A'   Coupe B-B'

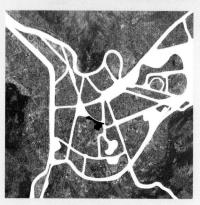

S333

Resumé

1990   Collaborative established in London as Studio 333

1997   The practice, S333 officially opened its office in Amsterdam, the Netherlands

Competitions and awards
2000   First prize (La Ville Forêt), Living in the Year 2000, Grenoble, France.

2000   First prize, Anglo-Dutch Award for Business Enterprise, UK/the Netherlands.

2000   First prize, regeneration of Tarling Estate, Tower Hamlets, London, in collaboration with Stockwoolstencroft Architects.

1999   Commended, Young Architects of the Year Award, UK.

1998   First prize, Vinex housing, Vijfhuizen, the Netherlands.

1996   First prize, Europan 4 housing competition, Manchester, UK.

1994   First prize (CiBoGa Terrain), Europan 3 housing competition, Groningen, the Netherlands.

1993   National Design Award for Urban Design, Karlsruhe, Germany.

1991   First prize, urban revitalisation, Samarkand, Uzbekistan, Commonwealth of Independent States.

Works in progress
2001   Private villa, Kliene Rieteiland, Amsterdam, the Netherlands.

2000–2003   Two urban blocks (housing, commercial, parking), Eschmarke, the Netherlands.

2000–2003   32 cliff houses, 18 row houses, Auckland, New Zealand. New town centre plan, Nieuw-Vennep, the Netherlands.

1998–2002   56 houses, Vijfhuizen, Haarlemmermeer, the Netherlands.

1997–2002   Two urban blocks (CiBoGa Terrain, first phase: Schots 1 and 2; housing, commercial, underground parking), Groningen, the Netherlands.

1997–   Recreational park 'Dutch Mountain'; (transformation of waste dump), Zaandam, the Netherlands.

2000–2005   New town centreplan, Nievw-Vennep, the Netherlands.

Burton Hamfelt | Chris Moller | Dominic Papa | Jonathan Woodroffe

123 +

SUSTAINING ARCHITECTURE IN THE ANTI-MACHINE AGE
Edited by Ian Abley and James Heartfield

PB 0 471 48660 4; £19.99; 279 x 217 mm; 240 pages; December 2001

The issue of sustainability is one of the guiding principles of contemporary architecture. Through a process of educational reform, changes to codes of conduct, and as a general promotion of sustainability in professional life through public statements, guidance and manifestoes, the Royal Institute of British Architects is currently instituting an environmental duty of care. However, although definitions of sustainability abound, they do not obviously translate into practice. Architectural practice will change, as it should, and this book anticipates what it will mean to be an architect now that sustainability is the measure of professionalism.

Sustaining Architecture in the Anti-Machine Age brings together contributions from a range of architects, journalists, academics and consultants, including high-profile figures such as journalist Martin Pawley and President of the Royal Institute of British Architects Paul Hyett. Their contributions approach sustainability from a wide variety of viewpoints and some take mutually exclusive approaches: rather than offering prescriptive guidelines, this book acts as a starting point that enables readers to come to their own conclusions. All options for sustainable development are covered, from high-density housing to dispersed village settlements, and from traditional methods to high technology. The thought-provoking texts are illustrated with carefully chosen example projects.

The book offers a 21st-century answer to two earlier seminal texts. In 1960 Reyner Banham wrote *Theory and Design in the First Machine Age*, exploring the formation of architectural attitudes in the early Modern Movement, where the focus was on pure form. Martin Pawley responded in 1990 with *Theory and Design in the Second Machine Age*, pointing out the practical factors which were coming into play – pollution, globalisation, resource depletion – and accusing architects of leaving the field to commercial interests. Since then, theory and design have ceded their architectural supremacy to the issue of sustainability. Architects are finding their roles reduced from one of creative imagination to one of mundane demand management. Clearly a balance is needed between the encouragement of inventive design, and the fostering of a responsible attitude to the environment. This book is a step along the way to achieving such a balance. ⌀ *Abigail Grater*

DESIGNING FOR A DIGITAL WORLD
Edited by Neil Leach

PB 0 470 84419 1; £24.95; 260 x 200 mm; 144 pages; January 2002

Digital technologies are playing an increasingly significant role in the ways that we live and work. No longer the subject of mere speculation and science fiction, they are having a profound impact on our material realities, and their effects extend into almost all aspects of life. But how exactly are they changing the discipline of architecture, and what are the lessons for the future?

This book features essays by a selection of internationally acclaimed figures from the fields of cultural theory, environmental planning, technology and design, and offers the first comprehensive view of the effects of digital technologies on the discipline of architecture. It provides a snapshot of expert opinion from those who are operating at the very forefront of innovative practices, and who are in a unique position to offer informed predictions as to the full potential of these technologies in the future. Ranging from a discussion of the nature of digital culture to the tectonics of computer-controlled fabrication and rapid-processing technologies, the book considers the entire spectrum of digital concerns that are beginning to influence architectural production.

Among the contributors are architectural firms and architects who have been featured many times in *Architectural Design* and other cutting-edge journals, including Lars Spuybroek (NOX), Hani Rashid (Asymptote), Mark Goulthorpe (dECOi) and Farshid Moussavi and Alejandro Zaera-Polo (Foreign Office Architects). Their writings explain their attitudes to their profession in the new digital age, and are accompanied by striking illustrations of their ground-breaking works. These are complemented by the more theoretical chapters by writers such as Sherry Turkle, Manuel DeLanda and Slavoj Zizek, all widely acknowledged as leading minds in their fields.

This book rethinks the relationship between humanity and technology, and challenges the antipathy to the computer that continues to dominate in certain architectural circles. It will appeal not only to architects, designers and students of related disciplines, but also to a constantly growing informed public interested in cultural theory, design and planning. ⌀ *Abigail Grater*

Book Reviews

CARCHITECTURE
edited by Jonathan Bell
August/Birkhauser, 2001, 128 pages, £24.00.

THE SPACE OF ENCOUNTER by Daniel Libeskind,
preface by Jeffrey Kipnis and afterword by Anthony Vidler,
Thames and Hudson (London), 2001, 229 pp, 200 colour illus., £22.95.

The automobile replaced the horse as man's best friend over 100 years ago and changed the environment, culture and humanity permanently. A number of recent publications have recognised this phenomenon and analysed the impact of the automobile on society. One of these is *Carchitecture*, edited by Jonathan Bell.

Horse-drawn transport required tracks, fields, stables, barns and coaching stations – modest accommodation in relation to the number of animals involved. Horses could be trained and fed, to be used as necessary for personal and public transport, and disposed of when they died without adversely affecting our surroundings. On the other hand the automobile, as an inorganic object, requires a vast amount of energy, manpower, finance and materials for its manufacture and a complex network of roads and motorways, filling stations, garages, parking lots and multistorey car parks. Cars pollute and litter the environment, consuming vast quantities of the earth's natural and finite resources. Nevertheless, the automobile has become a necessary modern entity, a cultural icon, a complex mirror of human behaviour and needs that reflects immediate technical and artistic advances. Cars not only demand buildings to accommodate them but also influence where they are located and their design, form and construction technology.

The contributors to *Carchitecture* explore and analyse the legacies of the automobile effect. The enormous rise in car numbers has caused a conflict within the human environment. The results are all around us: roads cut through countryside and cities, pollution changes our atmosphere, precious time is lost in traffic jams, material resources are used up to supply automobile manufacture and provide fuel, communities are divided by noisy routes and lives are lost in accidents. Having examined the history of this conflict, *Carchitecture* attempts to reconcile the automobile with the built environment by transferring technology and aesthetics from one to the other to improve the car's social status. Planning that would integrate the driving environment harmoniously with its surroundings is a possible way to progress. Architecture, urban design and cars will need to have the ability to adapt into an interchangeable process. This publication does not give answers to all the questions, but it opens the vital and necessary debate. ⌀

Ivan Margolius is the author of *Automobiles by Architects* Wiley-Academy, 2000.

In a world where the shallow is considered deep and the easy taxing, Daniel Libeskind's work shines out as a beacon of hope. His projects are disturbing, enigmatic yet always polemic. His work is often perceived as expressively mute at first glance. At second glance it reveals itself to the viewer and suddenly every line, every cut and every angle is steeped in meaning. It is always characterised by the creation of numerous spaces allowing the viewer to construct his or her own navigation through forms and ideas. One might argue that this is true of all architecture, yet with Libeskind the pieces seduce the viewer into his cabalistic, alchemic and intellectual world. His work reveals the strata below the normal anthropocentric geography of architecture.

This is the architecture of a 'modernism' that Joyce, Klee, Ernst and Schopenhauer would recognise. This is a different 'modernism' from that which passes for theory in a world of capitalist cheese-paring.

This book seeks to make connections between Libeskind's buildings and his early, formative projects – the Micromegas, the Chamberworks, Three Lessons in Architecture: the Machines and Theatrum Mundi. All works that were created between 1979 and 1985 are Libeskind's *prima materia*; the source of many of the graphic protocols and philosophical notions that characterise his oeuvre. This book is explicit in some but not all of these connections. Libeskind's writings are a web of associations and images and he is a master of enigma.

On one level this book declares Libeskind's love of the word, his commitment to architectural design needing to be more than visceral. It implies his love of the gap between the action and the word. In this nether zone between theory and practice Libeskind is very careful how he frames his work. For him the frame – whether the picture frame, the ideological frame, the graphic frame or the landscape frame – is of paramount importance. His vistas never privilege the singular but always the multiple; they twist back on themselves and flit across scales.

For me, this is the definitive Libeskind book so far published. I only hope that one day Libeskind will return to the twilight of the unbuildable for it is there, in the nether world of ideas, that he still has much to offer. ⌀ *Neil Spiller*

For this issue's Site Lines feature, Helen Castle, editor of *Architectural Design*, visits an innovative house only a stone's throw away from △'s offices in Ealing, West London.

There is nothing more uplifting than discovering a piece of contemporary architecture where you least expect it. Ealing in west London is 'sub-urban', close enough to town to have a London postal code but lacking the convenience or urban grittiness of a more central borough. Since moving to offices there in 1999 with its publishers, John Wiley & Sons, *Architectural Design* has found itself in an architectural never land, beyond the boundaries of most architects' cultural reference map — it is nigh impossible to entice anyone but a foreign ingenue to visit. Though Ealing is verdant, with greens and numerous small parks, making it a very pleasant place to live in, it is condemned by that most damning of British put-downs — that of being 'ordinary'. (In Sally Vickers' recent best-selling novel, *Miss Garnet's Angel*, the elderly heroine's dull existence is epitomised by the fact that she has spent a lifetime living in Ealing!). It therefore goes without saying that this area of west London does not have the same tradition of one-off modern houses as somewhere like Hampstead, which has managed to be both salubrious and 'arty' since the 1930s.

There is no doubt that in terms of planning and design the Brooke Coombes House is a ground-breaking project for its location. Its significance, however, extends far beyond its locality. As Catherine Burd of Burd Haward Marston Architects, the young practice that designed it (they have only been together two years) says, it is intended to be a very simple house: 'The office are interested in simple forms – reductivist in the sense that they reduce down to a clear diagram. We are most interested in building a clear description of a few ideas.' It is the very considered way that these few ideas are embodied in the house that makes it so innovative. Regarding it as a

'case study' house, the partners were intent on it providing an economical and expansive model for suburban family life. (The house is home to John Brooke and Carol Coombes and their three student-aged children, so its plan is tested in its most expanded form.) At the same time, BHM were also concerned that it took on contemporary notions of sustainability and energy conservation, and that it responded to its surroundings in a conservation area. The fact that it was being project-managed by Brooke and Coombes also meant it had to be straightforward to build, with a low-tech aesthetic that called upon readily available specialist technology rather than craftsmen.

The house departs most fundamentally from conventional domestic layouts through the designation of a large portion of the floor plan to a double-height glazed courtyard. Rather than being tacked on to the back of the house like most conservatories, it is placed to the left of the front elevation. The transparency that this affords allows the house to flout the usual residential delineation of front and back with its emphasis on the public street and the private rear garden. Both in terms of visibility and climate the courtyard is a transitory space, being neither strictly outside nor inside. It accommodates both the main entrance and a galvanised steel staircase which is the only means of reaching the bedrooms from the ground floor. This requires the occupiers hazarding a drop in temperature and the possibility of being seen from the street whenever they go up and downstairs to bed.

Opposite
The rear elevation of the Brooke Coombes House

Below
Ground-floor and first-floor plans of the house.

Below
Cross section of the Brooke Coombes House.

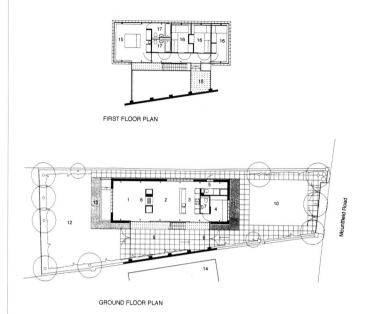

FIRST FLOOR PLAN

GROUND FLOOR PLAN

Mountfield Road

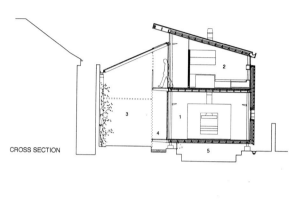

CROSS SECTION

It is, however, the way that the architects have responded to the courtyard in other aspects of the house's design that truly distinguishes the Brooke Coombes House as modern British domestic architecture. Like many British people, Brooke and Coombes were attracted to the idea of a modern house for its light and airy qualities. The only drawback to this in practice is the British climate, which makes us seek out the snuggest rooms in winter and huddle around the fire on chilly summer evenings. What BHM have succeeded in doing in the Brooke Coombes House is to combine a sense of lightness and airiness with cosiness and warmth. They have done this partly by orientating the house towards the courtyard, so that all the main views look on to it rather than to the front or the back. In contrast, the other three sides of the house appear as a solid block wrapped by a thick, highly insulated, terracotta-tiled wall which is carefully punctured with windows. The only large opening is a picture window that looks on to the west-facing garden from the downstairs living space. All the openings to the north are confined to narrow clerestory windows, which have also been carefully placed for their views. Whereas exposure to the north is minimised, contact on the south side is maximised. On both floors, the south 'wall' is made up of no more than large glazed sliding doors that can be opened up to effectively double the living space in warmer weather.

It is in the planning of space that the architects have excelled themselves, pulling off the seemingly undoable. Within the confines of a modest floor space, they have met all their clients' requirements, succeeding in including a study, cloakroom, utility room and open-plan living room with zoned areas on the ground floor and also four bedrooms and two bathrooms upstairs. (An additional storage area was created by John Brooke, who dug out an undercroft, which effectively acts as a reservoir for cool air in the summer, beneath the house.) Rather than evoking the decadent, empty sterility of 1990s Minimalism that we have recently become accustomed to, the interiors recall a distinctly British brand of Modernism. The attention to storage and built-in detailing recalls Erno Goldfinger in his own house at Willow Road in Hampstead. This is most effective where space is at a premium. The two children's bedrooms, which are north-facing, brought to mind my own experience of Denys Lasdun's student residents at the University of East Anglia in Norwich with their built-in furniture and a sense of privacy that is conducive to studying. Despite the discrepancy in the size of spaces on the ground and first floors, a continuity is retained through the detailing. The clerestory windows and a single shelf running beneath them are a recurring motif on both levels of the house.

What is clear is that this house offers a great deal to architects and house-owners in terms of the ideas that are played out in it. This has already been recognised at a metropolitan and a local level. When the clients opened their door for a single afternoon during the London Open House week, they had over 500 visitors. This has been followed up by a Civic Award from the Ealing Civic Society who evidently appreciate what they have in their midst. ⌂

Subscribe Now for 2002

As an influential and prestigious architectural publication, *Architectural Design* has an unrivalled reputation worldwide. Published bi-monthly, it successfully combines the currency and topicality of a newsstand journal with the editorial rigour and design qualities of a book. Consistently at the forefront of cultural thought and design since the 60s, it has time and again proved provocative and inspirational – inspiring theoretical, creative and technological advances. ∆ has recently taken a pioneering role in the technological revolution of the 90s ∆

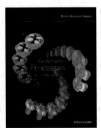

Contemporary Processes in Architecture
Guest-edited by Ali Rahim
ISBN 0471494402, June 2000 (profile 145)

The important precursor of *Contemporary Techniques in Architecture*, also guest-edited by Ali Rahim, *Contemporary Processes in Architecture* concentrates on the critical issue of process asking some of the most expedient and compelling questions of architectural practice today. It explores how contemporary processes, in the pursuit of creativity and fluidity, have become more abstract and experimental, attempting to overcome the pragmatic determinism attributed to more conventional working methods. It focuses on the work of architects who design with generative potentials, force fields and conceptual diagrams developed with the aid of high-end computer software packages. Featured architects include James Corner, Ed Keller, Kolatan/MacDonald Studio, Lars Spuybroek, Oliver Lang, Greg Lynn, Enrique Norten, OCEAN North, Reiser + Umemoto and UN Studio Van Berkel and Bos. Through elucidating texts and the potent imagery of process – many of the projects are illustrated stage by stage – effectively prefiguring the revolution that is about to happen in architectural design.

∆ Architectural Design

SUBSCRIPTION RATES 2002
Institutional Rate: UK £160
Personal Rate: UK £99
Discount Student* Rate: UK £70
OUTSIDE UK
Institutional Rate: US $240
Personal Rate: US $150
Student* Rate: US $105

*Proof of studentship will be required when placing an order. Prices reflect rates for a 2002 subscription and are subject to change without notice.

TO SUBSCRIBE
Phone your credit card order:
UK/Europe: +44 (0)1243 843 828
USA: +1 212 850 6645
Fax your credit card order to:
UK/Europe: +44 (0)1243 770 432
USA: +1 212 850 6021

Email your credit card order to:
cs-journals@wiley.co.uk
Post your credit card or cheque order to:

UK/Europe: John Wiley & Sons Ltd.
Journals Administration Department
1 Oldlands Way
Bognor Regis
West Sussex PO22 9SA
UK

USA: John Wiley & Sons Ltd.
Journals Administration Department
605 Third Avenue
New York, NY 10158
USA

Please include your postal delivery address with your order.

All ∆ volumes are available individually. To place an order please write to:
John Wiley & Sons Ltd
Customer Services
1 Oldlands Way
Bognor Regis
West Sussex PO22 9SA

Please quote the ISBN number of the issue(s) you are ordering.

∆ is available to purchase on both a subscription basis and as individual volumes

I wish to subscribe to ∆ Architectural Design at the **Institutional rate of £160.**

I wish to subscribe to ∆ Architectural Design at the **Personal rate of £99.**

I wish to subscribe to ∆ Architectural Design at the **Student rate of £70.**

STARTING FROM ISSUE 1/2002.

Payment enclosed by Cheque/Money order/Drafts.

Value/Currency £/US$

Please charge £/US$ to my credit card.

Account number:

Expiry date:

Card: Visa/Amex/Mastercard/Eurocard *(delete as applicable)*

Cardholder's signature

Cardholder's name

Address

Post/Zip Code

Recepient's name

Address

Post/Zip Code

I would like to buy the following Back Issues at £22.50 each:

∆ 154 *Fame and Architecture*, Julia Chance and Torsten Schmiedeknecht

∆ 153 *Looking Back in Envy*, Jan Kaplicky

∆ 152 *Green Architecture*, Brian Edwards

∆ 151 *New Babylonians*, Iain Borden + Sandy McCreery

∆ 150 *Architecture + Animation*, Bob Fear

∆ 149 *Young Blood*, Neil Spiller

∆ 148 *Fashion and Architecture*, Martin Pawley

∆ 147 *The Tragic in Architecture*, Richard Patterson

∆ 146 *The Transformable House*, Jonathan Bell and Sally Godwin

∆ 145 *Contemporary Processes in Architecture*, Ali Rahim

∆ 144 *Space Architecture*, Dr Rachel Armstrong

∆ 143 *Architecture and Film II*, Bob Fear

∆ 142 *Millennium Architecture*, Maggie Toy and Charles Jencks

∆ 141 *Hypersurface Architecture II*, Stephen Perrella

∆ 140 *Architecture of the Borderlands*, Teddy Cruz

∆ 139 *Minimal Architecture II*, Maggie Toy

∆ 138 *Sci-Fi Architecture*, Maggie Toy

∆ 137 *Des-Res Architecture*, Maggie Toy

∆ 136 *Cyberspace Architecture II*, Neil Spiller